GENERATION EUROPE

About Policy Network

Policy Network is an international thinktank and research institute. Its network spans national borders across Europe and the wider world with the aim of promoting the best progressive thinking on the major social and economic challenges of the 21st century.

Our work is driven by a network of politicians, policymakers, business leaders, public service professionals, and academic researchers who work on long-term issues relating to public policy, political economy, social attitudes, governance and international affairs. This is complemented by the expertise and research excellence of Policy Network's international team.

A platform for research and ideas

- Promoting expert ideas and political analysis on the key economic, social and political challenges of our age.
- Disseminating research excellence and relevant knowledge to a wider public audience through interactive policy networks, including interdisciplinary and scholarly collaboration.
- Engaging and informing the public debate about the future of European and global progressive politics.

A network of leaders, policymakers and thinkers

- Building international policy communities comprising individuals and affiliate institutions.
- Providing meeting platforms where the politically active, and potential leaders of the future, can engage with each other across national borders and with the best thinkers who are sympathetic to their broad aims.
- Engaging in external collaboration with partners including higher education institutions, the private sector, thinktanks, charities, community organisations, and trade unions.
- Delivering an innovative events programme combining in-house seminars with large-scale public conferences designed to influence and contribute to key public debates.

www.policy-network.net

GENERATION EUROPE

How Young Europeans Need to Step Up and Save Their Continent

Sandro Gozi

policy network

ROWMAN &
LITTLEFIELD
————INTERNATIONAL————

London • New York

Published by Rowman & Littlefield International Ltd.
Unit A, Whitacre Mews, 26-34 Stannary Street, London SE11 4AB
www.rowmaninternational.com

Rowman & Littlefield International Ltd. is an affiliate of Rowman & Littlefield
4501 Forbes Boulevard, Suite 200, Lanham, Maryland 20706, USA
With additional offices in Boulder, New York, Toronto (Canada), and Plymouth (UK)
www.rowman.com

British Library Cataloguing in Publication Data

A catalogue record for this book is available from the British Library

ISBN: PB 978-1-78660-792-8
ISBN: eBook 978-1-78660-793-5

Library of Congress Cataloging-in-Publication Data

Library of Congress Control Number: 2018930808

∞™ The paper used in this publication meets the minimum requirements of
American National Standard for Information Sciences—Permanence of Paper for
Printed Library Materials, ANSI/NISO Z39.48-1992.

Printed in the United States of America

CONTENTS

to Jo Cox

ACKNOWLEDGMENTS

I want to thank Francesco Gualdi, with whom I share politics, music and many hours of work each day, for his valuable contribution.

And thanks to François Lafond, who worked on the French edition of the book. With him, I have long shared European commitments and many initiatives here and beyond the Alps.

I also want to thank all the Policy Network team: they believed in the idea of this book and did a remarkable job in supporting it.

Together, we played as a team, as we should always do in Europe and for the Europe that we want.

SUDDENLY BREXIT

The first SMS woke me up at five in the morning. It was Matteo Renzi, the Italian prime minister at the time, asking me if I had "more data". I immediately understood that all the calculations, the exit polls, the forecasts and the data of the previous night meant nothing.

Brexit had just happened.

It was at that time on 24 June 2016 that I realised, for the first time, a member state had decided to leave the European Union. I immediately spoke with my friend Ed Llewellyn, then David Cameron's chief of staff at No 10. He confirmed that what seemed impossible just the night before had indeed happened, represented by the smirk of Nigel Farage and the rejoicing of Michal Gove and Boris Johnson.

That day I was in Luxembourg for the general affairs council. Brexit was on the agenda: based on the forecasts, we were supposed to be evaluating how to 'reset' the EU in the event of a remain win. But our forecasts were wrong; foreign affairs ministers began to arrive at the informal breakfast before the council, now a pointless occasion.

I remember doing an interview with BBC radio. They asked me what was going to happen after Brexit. I got by with a standard answer, but the reality was different: we knew we were entering uncertain and unknown territory. London did not seem prepared to handle the situation, and neither was Brussels. Obviously, 'Euro-destroyers' from all over Europe were rejoicing and hoping to use the exploit the apparent momentum caused by the Brexit vote.

I had never imagined a member state leaving the EU. My first doubts arose in Stockholm, a month before the referendum when, during a Policy Network conference, my friend Roger Liddle confessed to me that he was concerned about the result. I trust Roger's expertise on British politics and society, and his pessimism concerned me.

On various occasions, I have had the chance to live in the UK. The last time was in 1994. Those were the years of Cool Britannia, during the explosion of Britpop, of Tony Blair and New Labour: an era brilliantly built up by one of the brightest minds in British politics, Peter Mandelson. After the dark days of the 1970s and the conflicts of the Thatcher years, Britain seemed to be undergoing something of a rebirth, its 'soft power' growing. London during the 1990s was innovative and 'happening', acting as a magnet to attract young people from all over Europe.

I was among those young people. I lived in Rosebery Avenue in Islington (20 years later 75 per cent of voters in Islington voted to remain; a small comfort). I studied at the London School of Economics and played squash with Indian and Pakistani friends. At the LSE, my macroeconomics professor was Willem Buiter, who later joined the Bank of England monetary policy committee. I remember he often wore a white T-shirt with the drawing of a European tie, blue with 12 stars, under a black suit jacket. Back then, more than two decades ago, his lessons explained the need to introduce the single currency; but, at the same time, it was already clear that the eurozone was incomplete. All these issues quickly moved from economics to politics.

I witnessed a London that was undergoing a renaissance. Now London is completely transformed: I recently went back to LSE for a conference. The squash courts are now the, construction site of a new student office. I am sure it will be beautiful but at least for me, squash courts were much more romantic.

I have one simple question: what happened to the Great Britain I remember clearly? What has changed in the intervening years to cause a majority of Britons to vote to leave the EU?

NO EUROPE FOR OLD MEN

Right after the referendum, one figure stood out to me. Those who voted in favour of Brexit were older British citizens. 73 per cent of people aged 18-24 voted remain, as well as 62 per cent of those aged 25–34. People over the age of 45 voted leave, with the figure reaching its peak at 60 per cent among those older than 65. But Brexit won because British grandparents turned out in larger numbers than their grandchildren. That's democracy: if youngsters had really cared about the referendum, they could have gone to the polls in larger numbers. We feel lost in the face of such a decision. The results are not only different between young and old, but also between the cities and the provinces, without forgetting the divisions between the nations of the United Kingdom, with Scotland and Northern Ireland voting to remain and England and Wales to leave.

However, this is a somewhat superficial representation of the split between one generation that voted for its past and another that decided not to participate, to let someone else decide the future. This is not the case: the young have demonstrated that they believe in the EU because they were born and raised as European citizens. Because most of them have travelled through Europe, many have studied in universities in the continent and have friends located all over the EU. This is the Europe generation, the Erasmus generation, the generation that discovered the continent thanks to low-cost flights: the easyJet generation. The same easyJet that decided to leave London and move to make the EU, in this case Vienna, its base.

I focus on the generational issue because it is clear-cut. The results of the referendum tell us that among those people younger than 45, remain won. This means that those who were born after Britain joined the European Economic Community (EEC) in 1973 support the EU. It was the baby boomers who decided to leave the EU. Maybe because they recall a past that cannot be recaptured, they prefer to wallow in the dream of a 'Global Britain' (to use the words of Theresa May). But, nowadays, if a European country wants to be global, it needs to be part of the strongest union in the world, not on its own. The risk is that, outside of the EU, 'Global Britain' becomes 'Little England'.

However, the easyJet generation now has a great responsibility: too many young people took the EU for granted, failing to defend it enough during these tough moments.

TAKE BACK CONTROL

So why did the majority of Britons vote for Brexit? It is no secret that an increasing number of citizens feel that the EU is distant, irrelevant and sometimes even the enemy. Other than the differences between generations, Brexit gained most votes from the poorest and least educated. These are the social classes that were most affected by the financial crisis, that most fear the effects of globalisation, and do not hear answers to their problems.

Indeed, nowadays many believe globalisation is the root of all evil. Though the reality is different: thanks to globalisation, the global middle class (taking as middle class those earning between $10-50 per day) has increased by 70 per cent in the past decade. In China alone more than 200 million people joined the ranks of the middle class, in addition to 63 million in Latin America.

The problem is that we cannot say the same for the middle class in the west. According to the International Labour Organization (ILO), 19 out of 27 European countries experienced an impoverishment of their middle class between 2008 and 2011.

We have already seen the consequences of this in the US: Donald Trump won the election because he gave voice to this sense of loss. We can say that the Obama administration created millions of jobs and rebuilt the American economy, but this is not the point. As Bloomberg's David Ingold suggests, the disappearance of manufacturing jobs has taken away certainty from the working class, as traditional white-collar roles have become automated or moved offshore. While the American Democrats were praising the self-driving cars designed in Silicon Valley, Trump addressed the truck drivers afraid of losing their jobs. We saw how that ended.

This message was echoed in the power of the leave campaign's slogan: "Take back control". We have to take back control: control of our frontiers, of our currency, of our traditions. But first, we have to take back control of immigration. This is, without a doubt, one of the main reasons behind the victory of the leave campaign.

Leavers bet on a good number of unfounded promises. All the graphs and the statistics with which the remainers demonstrated that Brexit would greatly damage the UK economy were not worth a penny. The error of the remain campaign was failing to understand that the way people voted was emotional and irrational: not very British traits.

This was also a big mistake made by Cameron: he thought that a good campaign based on a deal with the EU would be enough to neutralise the extremists within his party.

I remember the various meetings I attended with Renzi: Cameron faithfully stuck to his belief that, with a good cost-benefit analysis, the rational British voter would make the 'right' choice. But after many years of Euroscepticism, that was never going to work: if you invest a lot of time attacking the EU and listing its defects, as many Tory remainers and the prime minister himself did during the renegotiation, then it is difficult to later convince people of the case for remain. On top of that, Jeremy Corbyn's behaviour did not help: his support for remain was, at best, lukewarm. This was critical: Brexit triumphed because of the great number of Labour voters that were won over by leave.

More than a year after the referendum, it is still not clear what the British government envisages for the future. For many months,

Theresa May hid behind the meaningless 'Brexit means Brexit' mantra. In January 2017, the prime minister plumped for a hard Brexit and then sought a mandate by calling a snap election for June. But the resulting loss of her parliamentary majority meant the situation has not become any clearer.

What was sold as a decision to take back control has instead plunged the UK into chaos. I still think that Brexit will be bad for everyone, but the UK itself will feel the worst effects. On the first anniversary of Brexit in June 2017, the British economic fundamentals were stark: the pound lost 14.5 per cent of its value, inflation increased by 2.4 per cent, the real growth rate decreased by 2.7 per cent and investment decreased by 0.9 per cent. To adapt a famous saying: Fog in the Channel, Britain cut off.

BREXIT AND BEYOND

I will always remember the image of one of the spontaneous demonstrations held by thousands of youngsters in Parliament Square a couple of days after 23 June. They were waving blue flags with the 12 stars and they were singing Hey Jude in support of the EU.

We need to bear them in mind as we start to build the future. London is not the UK, Paris is not France and New York is not the US. It is enough to look at the last census, which revealed that a third of London's residents were born outside the UK and that the city hosts 270 different nationalities, speaking more than 300 languages. We would probably be wrong to think these young pro-Europeans fully represent the country. However, what is clear is that they deserve an answer, because the decision on the future relationship between UK and EU will be of more relevance to the easyJet generation than to their Brexiteer grandparents. According to a survey on the first anniversary of Brexit, 85 per cent of young people aged 18-24 want to retain the right to live, travel and work in the EU. But these rights of EU citizenship will not be possible with a hard Brexit. Their future is uncertain, so we must find solutions, both for them and for EU citizens living in the UK whose future is similarly unclear. Every time I meet London's mayor, Sadiq Khan, I cannot help but think of the words he said the day after Brexit. Addressing European citizens living in London, Khan said with great simplicity: "You will always be welcome here."

As of today, nobody is able to predict what will happen during the Brexit negotiations. We cannot say with certainty what the relationship between EU and UK will be, since it will only be finalised at a later stage. Britain and Europe are friends and important allies; they will always have close relations on many issues. These include security, an issue that needs co-operation, especially with the threat of terrorism, which knows no territorial boundaries. It can strike at London Bridge, during a concert in Manchester, on the Promenade des Anglais in Nice or the Bataclan in Paris. It leads to insecurity, with our communities living in fear and demanding protection. If we want to succeed in solving this crisis in Europe, we need London on board, even if the city is no longer in the EU.

Brexit will be complicated. There will be many obstacles to success and the possibility of a storm. As I have always said, the negotiation does not provide an opportunity but, if we use common sense, a chance to limit the damage. However, this does not mean that there cannot be any positive consequences. For Britain? No, for the EU.

THE EUROPEAN SPRING

Brexit. Trump's election. The loss of the constitutional referendum in Italy. 2016 was a year of political defeats. But 2017 opened with even worse prospects in sight. In the Netherlands and France, elections were threatening to mark the demise of the EU. A win by Geert Wilders' populists or Marine Le Pen's National Front would have threatened the very existence of the union. But, exactly at the moment of maximum peril, Europe has come back and found renewed momentum.

Was there a specific moment at which this happened? On 25 March in Rome, we marked the 60th anniversary of the signing of the treaty of Rome. It was a symbolic event, though more political than expected. The declaration of Rome, signed by the 27 member states (Britain was absent), is the EU's first political reaction after the *annus horribilis* of 2016. It is substantive and launches innovative themes such as, for example, the establishment of a social union. More generally, the celebrations in Rome acted as an occasion to relaunch Europe: marches and pro-European demonstrations took place in many member states; young people waved the blue flag with twelve stars. The celebrations were the occasion for the re-discovery of a sense of European belonging.

Then Emmanuel Macron came onto the scene. There was no trace of him on the international political radar up until recently. I have had the chance to know him for a while, first as deputy secretary general at the Élysée palace and then minister for the economy and finance. I remember very well the day he called me three years ago and told me he was going to leave the Élysée to rebuild France. He wanted my help. This caught me by surprise. He asked me for suggestions of people to involve in his project. When I first met him at the ministry for the economy and finance, I found that he had chosen a student of mine at the College of Europe, Clément Beaune, as counsellor for European Affairs. He is a young man of the easyJet generation, bringing his pro-European vision to the Élysée palace.

Macron has had a stunning career, it goes without saying, but few predicted he would win the presidential election. As I wrote the French edition of this book, I was sure Macron, who at that time was deputy secretary general at the Élysée, was a young man to watch. I was convinced he was going to be part of the new generation in power. But when he left the Élysée, I had my doubts. I did not doubt him, because I know him. Macron has a great ability to predict political movements in advance and he is not afraid to make clear-cut decisions. My doubts were based on my knowledge of the French political system, and the fact I know the 'third way' in France is dangerous. But Macron decided to take the plunge and go his own way. He had the intuition to see a system in crisis, one that was slowly fading away.

Macron surprised everyone. He bet on a heavily pro-European election campaign, the likes of which we have not seen since Giscard d'Estaing. He was brave enough to face Marine Le Pen head on. He didn't let her set the agenda or give a nod and a wink to the National Front supporters. Instead, he laid out his own political agenda and he was proven right. His grand entrance at the Cour du Louvre to the strains of the Ode to Joy, as soon as his victory was assured, is one of those scenes that will always be remembered by France, and by Europe as a whole.

What does Macron's victory teach us? Not that all of the EU's problems have been solved. It will not be easy for the new president to carry through reform agenda, in France and, more generally, in Europe. He will find many obstacles along the way, because French society has conservative roots, and, above all, because the EU is slow moving, curbed by vetoes and the political calculations of its members.

However, Macron's election is a fundamental step towards the launch a new path in Europe. Not only did France reject a Europhobic candidate in the form of Le Pen, it also turned down François Fillon, who is lukewarm towards the EU. The country chose to bet on the EU, choosing faith, optimism, openness and innovation. The fact that this has happened in France, a country historically jealous of its national prerogatives, signals that an overhaul of the EU is not only possible but also probable.

It is too soon to say whether the populists have been definitively defeated or not. I do not believe so, but surely we have changed course. European society has the antibodies to resist those who want to smash it: the Netherlands demonstrated this. So did France. And the German elections of late September provided good results for the pro-European forces, from the Liberals to the Greens, although we should not underestimate the result of Alternative für Deutschland, the far-right party.

In this context, we seem, finally, to have moved past the financial crisis. European GDP is increasing, and with the prospect of a push toward new reforms, from this side of the Channel, we feel a little breeze in our sails. But we should always be careful not to lower our guard: new challenges await us on the horizon.

The last decisive battle against Europhobia will be in Italy, my country, in 2018. The Democratic party (PD) is the only pro-Europe party left in Italy, battling against the Le Pen-like, Lega Nord, and the anti-European Five Star Movement.

When I think back to my years in London, or to the many times that I have returned to the UK, I cannot help but feel a little wistful, and somewhat bitter. Brexit hurts economically, politically and also emotionally. We all imagined London fondly, as somewhere we could always go, for a weekend, for six months or for the rest of our life. The British will always be European, if not pro-Europe. No family is happy when a member leaves slamming the door.

So, is this our destiny? I am not sure. I did not agree at all with Theresa May's decision to opt for a hard Brexit early in 2017, one that would remove the UK from all EU structures, including the single market. That is why I welcomed her Florence speech in September, in which she sounded more open to constructive dialogue. I am also unconvinced by Jeremy Corbyn's campaign. For him, Brexit is a given and it is just a matter of going along with it. It is an unscrupulous tactic, which seeks to exploit the potential weakness of the Tories. It is justified, he believes, by the gains Labour made at the election. However, I must confess that seeing the Labour Party playing defence in this way – with the exception of Chuka Umunna, Pat McFadden, Emma Reynolds and a few others – pains me.

Recently, Donald Tusk, president of the European council, responded, to those who asked if Brexit might be reversed, with a reference to John Lennon: "Who knows? You may say I am a dreamer, but I'm not the only one."

No, Tusk is not the only one. British friends, the door of the EU will always be open. Sooner or later, our paths will cross again. And, if sooner, it will be better for everyone if – to use another musical reference – the days of Brexit are, as Kasabian sing: simply forgotten.

49 BOULEVARD VOLTAIRE

49 Boulevard Voltaire is not the Bataclan's address, which is actually located at number 50. Rather it is where, as a young European, free and without fear, I lived for one of the many years I spent in Paris. Just like Valeria Solesin, I studied at the Sorbonne. Valeria has left us now, a victim of terrorism – Italy and Europe will miss her. Back then, I would never have imagined that 20 years later monsters would pass through the very same streets I roamed everyday as a carefree student, attacking our freedom, hating the civil liberties which we have achieved, wanting to instil fear in us and to paralyse our society.

Why did those Islamist terrorists choose the Bataclan as the target of their insane massacre? Because inside that club, listening to rock music, they found hundreds of youngsters – young people from all over Europe and, indeed, beyond – gathered together because of their shared love of music and their desire to have fun. They form part of a generation that is completely different to all the other generations preceding them: the Europe generation, the Erasmus generation, the easyJet generation. They have travelled to study and they study to travel. They have made friends in a number of foreign countries, they have learned various different languages and they have discovered different cultures. They are free because they are European and European because they are free.

AN INTUITION ABOUT THE FUTURE

The Erasmus programme is the most astute creations of the EU. The establishment of a network of exchange programmes to provide opportunities to study abroad for as many students as possible was a magnificent idea, which opened the doors of our countries and universities to these young people.

The more I think about it, the more impressed I am by this sta- tistic: since the launch of the Erasmus programme in 1987, more than nine million European youngsters have reaped its benefits, experiencing new realities, new worlds, and new cultures. It stands in such stark contrast to the millions of European young people who, also in our recent history, perished in the trenches that separated our states and peoples. At home, I still keep the photo of my grandfather, Giacomo, a very young *bersagliere* soldier who fought in the first world war. Next to his photo is his medal for valour as well as the bullet from the Austrian sniper, probably a boy just as young as he was, that maimed him and left him limping for the rest of his life. In contrast, I, at the tender age of 17, was already roaming all over Europe together with many other youngsters from various countries. And now, it is almost impossible for me to explain to my children that when I was their age there were two Germanies.

Nowadays millions of young people participate in the Erasmus programme. Young men and women who find it just as normal to attend university, do voluntary work, join exchange programmes or play sport in Bologna as they would in Bruges or Barcelona; young people who communicate via WhatsApp in French or in English and who have friends they can go and stay with in various different countries.

Young men and women have taken up the opportunity to study in every corner of Europe – and not just study. If we glance at the statistics published by the European commission, we find that since 1987 over a million babies were born as a result of encounters that occurred thanks to the Erasmus programme. Babies that, without a doubt, have blue blood with golden stars coursing through their veins. When I lived in Paris in 1994, I went to listen to Umberto Eco's inaugural lecture at the College of France. He argued that Europe would come about naturally from the countless couples who would meet thanks to the Erasmus programme and whose children would have Europe imprinted in their DNA. He was right and, if Erasmus has one limitation, it is that it was not expanded, with adequate funding, to all university students. We must work to achieve this goal so that everyone will be able to have this opportunity, and the incentive to undertake it. My proposal is very simple and I stressed it during the celebrations of the 30th anniversary of Erasmus+. We must increase its funding tenfold. If four million students have participated in the programme over the past 30 years, then in the next 10 years, that must be increase to 40 million, 10 times more than the original number.

Thanks to all of this, Europe has become a part of our everyday life and if now we take it for granted, let's try to look back to the year when the Erasmus programme was launched. The Berlin Wall still stood, we had to show our passports at European borders and those who travelled with lira in their pockets had to exchange them as soon as possible for marks, pesetas or, as in my case, francs. I myself am part of this Erasmus generation, being one of the pioneers I described earlier.

The academic year I spent in Paris in 1989–1990, just as the Berlin Wall was starting to crack, was a fundamental one for not only my university career and my future profession but also for my life more widely. Low-cost airlines did not exist at the time, because we were yet to create the single market. In order to travel to Paris I used to catch the Galilei train, which departed from Florence and stopped in Bologna at around 11pm, arriving at the Gare de Lyon the next morning at around 7am. I knew France well, having studied French language and literature. I had travelled there since the age of 17, and

I continued to live there and visit often, for many years thereafter. Of all the experiences I have had the good fortune to have, more than any other, that year in Paris as a law student at the Sorbonne allowed me to better understand a rich culture and to improve my French (which, as it did for my children who were born in Brussels, became my second language). Above all, it allowed me to live the same life as that of any other student in France. During some of the first classes, I had to explain to some professors, those who were ill informed about what the Erasmus programme was all about, what I was doing there – us students from the University of Bologna and from the Complutense University of Madrid. However, for the most part I was an Italian who lived in France as a Frenchman, or rather a European in Europe. Afterwards I lived in Paris for several years. Each time I return, I remember that, without that experience at the Sorbonne, my life would have been completely different.

It was at that time that I learned about the drama of the Kurdish people, thanks to my close friendship with Bakhtiar Amin. At the time a Swedish political refugee and fellow student at the Sorbonne, Bakhtiar went on to become the first minister for human rights in post-Saddam Iraq. Those weekends spent with him at the Kurdish Institute in Paris, just like my unforgettable trip to Diyarbakır, in Turkey, really meant a lot to me, giving me an 'insider' view of the tragedy endured by persecuted minorities. François Mitterrand was president at the time, and therefore the politics I experienced was very different to that of the first Italian republic. In general, politicians were more open to international issues and, above all, to a European debate, or at least to an intense deliberation of the role of France in Europe. A few years later I found myself amongst the 'yes' militants – or the '*oui*' faction – fighting in favour of the Maastricht treaty, together with the French minister for European affairs at the time, Élisabeth Guigou, and following with apprehension that historic debate between Mitterrand and Philippe Séguin in the magnificent amphitheatre of the Sorbonne. What was I doing there? Well, where else would I be? They were discussing and deciding on my future too. They were discussing Europe.

NATURALLY EUROPEAN

Europe and Erasmus, Erasmus and Europe. What's new about a programme that has been going for 30 years? This point is best considered within the context of all that has happened in the last few months. In Europe, we now see at the forefront of political and economic decision-making members of the Erasmus generation, the generation that was raised within and trained by the Erasmus programme: my generation. This not only means that the Erasmus programme has been a vital tool to increase the knowledge, and the experience, of many young Europeans, but that many of these youngsters who once packed their bags to travel around Europe for a year have in the meantime grown into today's European leaders. I do not use the word 'European' by chance: the goal of the European commission led by Jacques Delors when the Erasmus programme was launched (which, by the way, was the brainchild of the excellent Italian *fonctionnaire* Domenico Lenarduzzi) was not simply to mould a new generation of Italian, French, German, British or Portuguese students. The goal that, in my opinion, has been reached was to mould a new generation of Europeans, capable of studying anywhere, of working anywhere, of living anywhere within the EU and of governing their own countries with the knowledge of this new European political and social dimension. All this was founded on a basic principle: whoever has travelled and lived in Europe, could not help but love Europe. Thus, today there is an entire generation of politicians, economists, technical experts and intellectuals ready to believe in Europe, whose lives and work are all about Europe.

I can just imagine the first objection to these statements: all this talk of new recruits when, in reality, it's always the same people in charge. This book also serves the purpose of reminding us that this is not quite the way things are. Probably for the first time in the history of the EU, a new class of European politicians hold top office posts within their own national governments as well as within the European institutions. This is also my generation: European because we were raised and trained in a continent that was free and becoming more united and integrated. A ruling class that is 'naturally European' and is now being put to the political test within their own national governments.

I have already discussed Emmanuel Macron, so I will start with the man who would, without doubt, have been put to the test in France if a heart attack had not taken him from us aged just 42. I refer to Olivier Ferrand, one of the most brilliant young French politicians of his generation, who rethought the meaning of French socialism and helped bring it back to power under François Hollande. Olivier was, and remains, a point of reference for an entire generation of young progressive European politicians. Among them Manuel Valls, who until a few months ago, was prime minister of France, naturally stands out. Born in Barcelona, he has lived all his life in France, but only acquired his French passport at the age of 18. One brilliant politician in Valls' government was Najat Vallaud-Belkacem, the minister for education.

If we turn to Germany, the best example is Michael Roth, the minister for European affairs, who was born in Hesse, just a few kilometres from the border that divided Germany in two. His political life has focused on fighting for a Europe that no longer contains such dividing lines. Then we can turn our attention to Portugal, where António Costa's government is facing difficult challenges. His minister for education, Tiago Brandão Rodrigues, not yet 40 years old, with a background in research, studied in both Spain and Great Britain. This generation hails from all corners of Europe. In Madrid, we have Albert Rivera, the brilliant leader of the new liberal and pro-European *Ciudadanos* (Citizens) party. In Malta, we find an excellent young Labour prime minister, Joseph Muscat, who again recently won elections, while in the far north, in Sweden, we find my friend Mikael Damberg, the minister for enterprise, with whom I regularly cross paths at the annual Policy Network reunions. Another fellow Europeanist and confident Erasmus alumnus is the liberal Xavier Bettel, prime minister of Luxembourg. In addition to being very smart, he is also very funny, which never hurts.

I mention just a few of the politicians I have had the pleasure to work with. Their story is the story of hundreds of thousands of young people who live in Europe today. They study in European universities, travel and get to know each other. They are yet unaware that amongst them lies a future president of the European commission, commissioner or minister.

It is incredibly fitting that the Erasmus generation, those who, more than any other generation, have lived Europe from the inside, and who know Europe's potential and positive aspects, find themselves with a real opportunity to change things at a time when Europe has been devastated by two tragic crises. First is the external crisis, which comes from the threat posed by terrorists that want to destroy our lives and who, perhaps, realise even more than we do, how real our union really is – a union of liberty, values and opportunities. Then there is the internal crisis, which is less obvious and cruel perhaps, but certainly no less dangerous. This is our own citizens' declining trust, and surging nationalist extremist movements who offer easy solutions that, in reality, would serve only to aggravate our problems: exiting the EU, dismantling Schengen, abandoning the euro, renouncing our civil liberties or rejecting our solidarity with one another. These are just the top five false solutions that, by focusing on 'what could have been', would drive us towards internal crisis and global irrelevance, instead of facing our common challenges together.

The challenges we are face are huge. On the one hand, we must mend the relationship between European institutions and citizens and rebuild the trust that has been lost in the last few years. On the other, we must stand strong in our response to the threats we face on our borders, but without forgetting our fundamental values.

We must avoid the easy solutions that would fan the flames of fear, extremism and xenophobic populism. In the short term, a politician might gain a few points in the polls if they chose this course. There is a great deal of anger in our society, and stirring it up could certainly boost one's popularity a little. However, the politics of anger only injects poison into our society; it weakens it, divides it, and corrodes it from the inside. Our course should be a different one. We can leave that to the likes of Nigel Farage, Matteo Salvini and Beppe Grillo. Difficult open seas await us. We can expect to encounter the false chants of the Eurosceptic sirens who aim to lure our ship towards the rocks. However, we can be secure in the knowledge that this is not the future that awaits us. It will no doubt be hard. It will also be costly. But our generation tore down the barriers of language, culture and education, and never stopped dreaming of a united states of Europe. Thinking back to the era of the founding fathers inspires us to believe we are living in the time of those children who will be founding our union. Our thoughts must be clearer than ever, based on hope, not anger. We must have the courage to take decisions to build a Europe of opportunity, not one of bureaucratic limits based on the politics of fear.

This generation is different from the one that preceded us, some of whom are still in government, even in important states. The generation before ours is sandwiched awkwardly. Unlike the founding fathers of Jacques Delors, Helmut Kohl, François Mitterrand, Giorgio Napolitano and Romano Prodi, they did not experience the war or the immediate postwar years because they were born too late, but neither did they know the Europe of Erasmus, because they were born too early. They are the baby boomers who lived through the greatest period of growth in the west, who benefited from incredible opportunities but who have not thought about what kind of Europe to leave for the next generation. This in between generation is the one that has held the union together over the last 10 years. I could list them by name, but ultimately it is not important.

Those who brought the EU through this spiral of technocracy and austerity did so for a very simple reason: for them, Europe is not a beacon of hope, a way out of the horrors of war or a great opportunity to be experienced. To them, it is simply the best of all the available options. There was no sign of hope among all those absurd financial constraints that ended up forcing a number of our member states and their citizens to their knees. Because of this, since Maastricht there have been no further moves towards political unity.

Because of this, the first Greek crisis was mismanaged through selfishness, short-sightedness and mistrust, and at great cost to the Greeks, as well as many other Europeans.

Here lies the scale of our challenge.

In 2017, we lost Helmut Kohl, one of the giants of European history. At his memorial in the European parliament, Emmanuel Macron used words that left a mark on me. After paying respect to the greatness of Kohl and of his generation, Macron underlined that one day history will judge our generation as well. "History will harshly judge the concessions we made to short term calculations, to national self-interest and the easy choices we have made," the president declared. I could not agree more.

THE COURAGE TO ACCEPT ONE'S RESPONSIBILITIES

The new generation is not being called upon to govern Europe as though this were some mere administrative exercise. When faced with a time of change, budget cuts and insecurity about the future, we have the duty to change Europe's course. What does all this mean? On the one hand, it is our time, and therefore we must have the courage to accept the challenge and the responsibility that this brings with it. On the other hand, we also know that, if we fail, we will have only ourselves to blame. No matter what the outcome, we will have run out of excuses. There will be no one left to blame for the mistakes we may make.

The aim of this story is to make an appeal for Europe, because I am ever more convinced that I belong to a European generation capable of transcending boundaries. But when one speaks of new generations in government, I cannot help but glance towards a photograph I have. We find ourselves in Piombino in April 2009, a group of Italians in their thirties and forties who met to try to and understand what needed to be done to move forward out of this rut. In reality, we are only 'relatively' young but, with a few exceptions, none of us had held any notable government or administrative positions at the time. At most, there were a few parliamentarians and mayors among us. What brought us together was a shared desire to change the status quo, looking towards Italy and Europe, with none of us afraid to play our role and to assume the responsibilities required to bring about such a change.

It was a chance meeting, following a forum organised by *L'Unità* immediately after the resignation of Walter Veltroni as leader of the Italian Democratic Party (PD). In *L'Unità*'s headquarters, after a debate that lasted all afternoon, we looked at each other and thought: but why don't *we* try to be the proponents of the change we want for Italy? Do we see ourselves in this role? We were all in Piombino simply by chance, but our meeting was anything but casual. It was proof of a great need to affect change – in a country where we continuously change the party symbols but where their leaders remain the same. We were very proud of the symbol of our party, but we wanted to change those who led it. Thanks to this, the European sentiment was very strong, because the experiences learned from other countries showed that, at 35 or 40 years of age, one could in fact govern a nation. We could see that many of our peers already held high office in both national governments and European institutions. At the end of the day, it was not, and it is not, a matter of age. What makes a difference when you have a political project is linking your to political action within the right dimension – the transnational dimension. One must break free from the shackles of the unwritten rules of one's own politics, Roman or Parisian or whatever they may be, and instead think as a European or act at the scale of the problem you wish to solve, be it within your local city or within our union.

Looking at that group photo six years down the line, our first bet has been won. What are the *piombini* doing today? (*Piombini* being how someone ironically described Marianna Madia, who is today our minister for public administration.) Ivan Scalfarotto is deputy minister for economic development. Debora Serracchiani is the president of the Friuli-Venezia Giulia region and deputy secretary of the PD. Andrea Romano, Irene Tinagli and Pippo Civati have all since been elected into parliament, while Anna Paola Concia was already serving in parliament at the time of the meeting. Andrea Orlando, now minister for justice, dropped by our meeting on the first day. One of those absent from the family photo, but only because he left early, was our future leader, Matteo Renzi. Replacing the old with the new, changing the party with the emergence of new leaders like Maria Elena Boschi and Luca Lotti and finally, the biggest challenge of all, governing the nation, changing Italy and driving change in Europe – without his leadership we would not have won that bet.

Now we have to face together the other bets we wish to win. This generation has tested itself with the responsibilities of government, we have won many battles, but we lost a crucial test: the constitutional referendum in December 2016. It was a big occasion, not just for us politicians, but for the whole country. Many reforms, which we had discussed for many years, were at stake. This time we could not paper over the cracks: the issue we have tried to tackle will not fade away. Sooner or later, the whole nation will have to deal with Italy's crumbling institutions and their many dysfunctions.

Our opponents argued the constitutional and electoral reforms were part of an 'authoritarian tendency'. The proposed system would have provided the opportunity for the winning party to gain an absolute majority, due to the presence of a run-off. How could this could be considered authoritarian? Transforming a minority into a majority has happened in France since 1958: it means solid and stable governments and accountability. Macron brilliantly won the presidential election with the backing of only 24.01 per cent of voters. Personally, I am envious of the French system.

Putting to one side the result of the referendum, one thing that stands out for me is the fact that, in less than five years, that group, and other 30 to 40 year olds with them, rose to power in Italy thanks, above all, to the courage and determination of Renzi. It was achieved in an improvised manner, in the only way that it could be successful – by breaking with the past. This was a more forceful break than ever before. It was a more powerful change than normal, because our nation is not used to real change. We navigate in the shadow of someone else until the arrival of the new. For example, in Italy we have 13,000 fully qualified professors of which only six – that's right, six – are under the age of 40. In other European countries, generations come to positions of responsibility and then step down, in a natural cycle, across politics, the public sector, education and so on.

We have all heard overtures of action in the past, but this time it actually took place. An entire generation in Italy took the bull by the horns and chose to confront the challenges of government. Or, to use a stronger expression, the challenges of power.

'Power' is a difficult word. One's natural reaction is to fear it, to consider it dangerous. Furthermore, in Italy, we have always associated power with arbitrary judgement or opaque decision-making. But this is all wrong. We should not be afraid of power, because our guiding principle is to improve the society within which we live, to improve our nation and to improve our Europe. This is why, while we studied and travelled around Europe, we all returned home. It is because of this that each one of us lives as a politician but make politics only a small part of our lives. I have always admired a statement made by Dag Hammarskjold, the former UN secretary general: 'Only he deserves power who every day justifies it'.

Most importantly, the left should not be afraid to utter the word 'power'. This is key to the transformation that we are bringing forth in Italy as well as in Europe. A new generation of leaders is affirming itself because it is absolutely determined to radically change today's society. In order to do so, the challenge of government is, first and foremost, a question of responsibility.

All too often in Italy – though France could be another good example – the left has proven itself incapable of facing the challenges of government. Instead, it has preferred to entrench itself in irresponsible schemes, abandoning government (as in France) or allowing it to fall (as in Italy) to then abandon the country to the right. Better to lose power than to lose oneself, or so they thought. But that does not work. We will never manage to implement our plans if we do not enter the field and play the game. We must take risks and launch new and innovative ideas. The left that refuses the test of government, and thus of power, renounces the opportunity to change society, and is therefore no longer true to itself. We must accept the challenge, knowing that nothing lasts forever. We must affect as much change as possible while we have the opportunity to do so, without living in the fear of the day when we will no longer have that opportunity.

MOVING AWAY FROM CRISIS MANAGEMENT

No one told us that our reawakening would be so rude.

We fell asleep one evening in November 1989, thinking it would be the lightest sleep we would ever experience. That evening I was at home in Bologna, studying labour law. Faced with images of the Berlin Wall crumbling before my very own eyes, I stopped what I was doing and began calling my friends to see what was the best way to travel by train to the city that was finally being reunited. At the time we did not have access to websites though which one could easily plan such a trip with a few clicks of the mouse. We imagined a future based on democracy, rights and freedom, and we thought that, once achieved, it would last forever.

My generation was the first not to experience war. As children, we heard adults speak of that era, and we grew up thinking we would put a definite end to what had been, freeing ourselves from the chains of a burdensome past to aspire to greener pastures.

We believed that through Europe we could achieve anything. Our continent had suddenly become the world's largest experiment in innovation and opportunity, following the healing of the wound that caused by the Berlin Wall. In fewer than five years, Europe had reunited Germany, introduced a single market, launched a single currency, and forged a new path for the generations to come.

We were encouraged to travel and study abroad; we opened up our borders and extended a hand to the countries of the former Eastern bloc. If not quite part of history in the making, we at the very least felt on the right side of history. And we felt that the seeds that we had sowed in the nineties – the ideas, the policies, the actions – would yield fruit capable of facing any challenges we confronted in the long run.

DEPARTING FROM WHERE?

The awakening was, however, a rude one. Since we had predicted that all would be well, when we began receiving bad news, we did not react decisively but started looking inwards, becoming insular. The events of 9/11, Iraq, the failure to adopt the European constitution and, finally, the onset of the financial crisis, were exacerbated by what the EU failed to do. We paid an unacceptable price, an unfair price that could easily have been avoided but which we paid because of a policy of crisis management that prioritised national self-interest.

The Europe we have experienced in the last few years is not the Europe we dreamed of: that beacon of democracy for all the countries freed from the yoke of the Soviet bloc. The nightmares that precede the awakening are usually always the ugliest. For us, they were the terrorist attack on the satirical newspaper Charlie Hebdo and, a few months after that, the attack at the Bataclan and the Stade de France. Paris was hit at its heart; Europe was hit at its heart. In the meantime, hundreds of others perished at sea, drowning in the Mediterranean. Europe had transformed from cradle of civilisation to a cemetery of indifference and of fear.

Certainly, one must react to events. Never before these past few years have I thought so often of Harold Macmillan's famous words to a young journalist in 1958. When the British prime minister was asked the largest problem he had overcome during his first year in Downing Street, he replied "Events, dear boy, events." The attacks at Charlie Hebdo and the Bataclan are our 9/11, both more dangerous and powerful than the tragic attacks of 2004 and 2005 in Spain and Great Britain. On those occasions, the attacks were aimed at public transport, with the clear intention of killing as many people as possible. The Islamist terrorists did not care who the dead were: male or female, Christian, Jewish, Muslim or atheist. It was only important that the victims were westerners.

Ten years later, sadly, the locations of the attacks have become more pointed. The terrorists wanted to hit the satirical newspaper because it mocked religion – but, in reality, it mocked everything, because in our society it was free to do so. In the more recent attacks, terrorists brought death and terror to places of fun – a nightclub, a stadium, restaurants. The symbolism in this is clear. Their goal was to attack the very roots of European society, the places where we have achieved the most freedom; places where we are free to laugh and have fun because, in a secular society, taboos should not exist. The attack on Friday 13 November 2015 at the Bataclan was aimed at a generation that is free, multilingual and cosmopolitan – the Erasmus generation. The place was violently attacked as 130 innocent young men and women were massacred by fanatics who were even younger than their victims.

How the was the attack on Charlie Hebdo even possible? How was the attack on the Bataclan possible? Why is Europe suddenly finding itself doubled over in fear, facing threats not only outside its borders but also within them, a victim of her very own political short-sightedness? The march of world leaders through Paris a few days later, in which I had the great honour of participating, was just the first step. When, on 11 January 2015, I marched on Boulevard Voltaire, I would never have imagined that, just a few months later, another even greater tragedy would unfold on that very same boulevard. A street where I had lived in my years in Paris, a street that has now become a symbol of something we have not yet understood, and that is now threatening the very fabric of our existence.

If we wish to rise above and face these many threats to our society, we must leave behind the EU we currently have and head towards the Europe we wish to have.

Above all, we must return to being the union that followed the fall of the iron curtain when, on 1 May 2004, 10 countries joined us after many years under the yoke of the Soviet Union. I will always remember a very intense debate held at the University of Vilnius in 2003 when, in opposition to some in the audience who opposed joining the EU in the name of sovereignty, other students reacted by saying: "today we choose freely and democratically to join the European Union; we do not recall the day when our people voted to join the Soviet Union." Such declarations of hope were daily occurrences for an EU that was still under construction. By contrast, we do not want a union that constantly mourns deaths in the seas off of Lampedusa and is unable to take the decisions necessary to avoid these tragedies from recurring every few months.

To achieve this we have to be able to think not only about the present, but, more importantly, about the future. We need to regain control of our common future, as Europeans. That future which the nationalist extremists want to steal from us. We must debunk the myth that our problems are always caused by the EU. It is a convenient scapegoat but in truth, often the EU holds the solutions we are looking for. The problem is that we do not realise this. Or, as I believe, we simply lack the will to construct a union in the areas where it unfortunately does not yet exist.

BEYOND EMERGENCY AND AUSTERITY

In 2007, despite years of confrontations, mistakes, and rifts, trust in the EU was at 57 per cent. Ten years later, that trust has decreased by exactly 20 points and currently stands at 37 per cent. During this period, we experienced the worst economic crisis our continent has known since at least 1929. Many scholars actually claim that the economic crisis of 2008 was even worse in relative terms.

Let's be clear, we did not create this crisis. It was a wholly American creation that reached a global scale, crashing our markets and hitting our economy harder than ever, simply because it found us fragmented and unprepared. The financial crisis transformed into a socially devastating economic crisis, which has today become more of a political crisis. It may sound absurd, but today the United States has emerged out of this crisis and is heading towards economic growth of five per cent, while we are only now starting to experience the first signs of recovery. After years of austerity, we should breathe a sigh of relief that things are looking up. However, we cannot help but ask ourselves a fundamental question: why was the EU incapable of handling the economic crisis? Its inability to manage it is what led its citizens to lose their trust in Europe.

There is no clear-cut reply to this question, but there is an explanation that I do find convincing, that Europe was unable to depart from the logic of crisis management that has guided it throughout these years. It freed itself from the Berlin Wall, it won its battle for freedom, but then became a prisoner to the politics of crisis management, held tightly within the jaws of selfishness and mutual mistrust. Was there a crisis? Certainly, but by simply patching up the leak we did not think of how to respond to what would happen next. The management of the euro crisis in the summer of 2011 is a blatant example of this. We put the brakes on what could have been a devastating crisis that could have led to the forced abandonment of our common currency, and thus to the disintegration of the European project. However, as soon as we managed to save what was salvageable, we returned to our bad old habits with our management of the Greek crisis. Instead of responding in time with adequate instruments, European leaders allowed the Greek situation to get worse. And it soon became another emergency to solve.

Let's look at the EU budget for the years 2014-20, which is valued at just €960bn; less than one per cent of Europe's GDP. The budget may have appeased those who wanted less Europe, but certainly not those who wanted more Europe. It is ridiculous that we fill European treaties and council communiques with so much hypocrisy, full of language on common political objectives, with new objectives always more ambitious than the last ones, but then we do not give the necessary tools to the EU to achieve these objectives. Along with Emma Bonino and some other parliamentarians, I requested, Italy consider perhaps using its veto for the first time. However, the request fell on deaf ears. This was partly because the Italian government of the day, like all the others before it for that matter, bartered to achieve a relatively small advantage (in our case concerning cohesion policy) which it then presented to its supporters as an historic achievement. It was also partly because no government has ever shown a sense of the long-term planning that is required, as well as the courage necessary to block a decision – in this case, it was a wrong decision because it was a hypocritical one – in the name of a fairer Europe. Once again, crisis management dictated their actions. Once the crisis passed, we returned to business as usual, and thus remained constantly under the remorseless logic of crisis management.

However, this leads us to another identifiable problem, and that is that business as usual as conducted by the EU over the last few years has been austerity. An austerity of ideas and values more than financial austerity – an austerity that ruled our hearts and minds as much as our wallets. How did we manage to find ourselves lost in such a labyrinth from which we are only now emerging after some enormously difficult years?

It came about because we allowed a zealous technocracy to accumulate more and more power and centralise the European institutions, while some political leaders showed short-sightedness and an inability to think beyond nation-based psychological schemes. To be clear, some are guiltier than others. However, the end result is that, over the last few years in Brussels, an ideology has taken shape that derives its mantra from financial algorithms and derives its reason from their blind application. This ideology is interpreted and applied with the admirable determination of technocrats who are out of touch with the realities of individual countries and societies and by sherpas forced to participate in lengthy nocturnal summits, without the necessary democratic control exercised by parliaments. European and national technocrats have been the main players in the EU for at least the last decade.

They have abandoned, for the most part, the community method of doing things – which in the past allowed the EU to be born and to achieve great results – thus denying all possibility of using the path of democracy and transparency to react to modern crises and to complete the union. This is how we arrived at many of the problems we are faced with today. Our treaties have proven insufficient to achieve our goals: during the crises, ways were even invented to circumvent the institutions and democratic oversight, and thus the common rules and transparency that had previously been guaranteed were absent. Instead of moving forward, we retreated.

The crises harmed democratic and institutional processes, as I witnessed first hand at the European summit of 12 July 2015. At that summit our leaders entered the Justus Lipsius building, the seat of the European council in Brussels, on Sunday at 4pm, after the finance ministers had assured us there were only a 'few square brackets left to be ironed out' (or two political knots to untie). Those knots turned out to be as heavy as marble and it took over 17 hours to remove them and, with them, the threat of Grexit (a Greek exit from the eurozone) and thus the disintegration of Europe. The leaders left that building on Monday morning at 9.30am. That night clearly showed that the method used by the EU to manage crises did not work; that the way we govern the euro needed to change; and that our leaders had to show some leadership, setting out clearly the fundamental goals they wished to achieve rather than getting caught up in discussing the details of Greek pharmacies or bakeries.

I think that, at that moment, only the heads of state and government fully realised the seriousness of all that was going on. I clearly recall that other European officials present that night, immersed as they were in this technocratic system, were unable to make the distinction between political choices – those which really meant something – and the technical rules to be resorted to in order to achieve those decisions, and those rules which are not necessarily a means to an end. Reform of the (non) governance of the euro is the most urgent structural reform that is required. We have already wasted too much time.

No greater error could have been committed than adopting the policy of austerity. Not only did it fail to help the EU member states emerge from the crises, but, in so doing, it served to diminish the trust its citizens had in the union to a miserly 37 per cent. This caused great damage to our nations from both an economic and a social point of view. Let's briefly consider the Greek case. The Greek governments have been responsible in large part for mismanaging public funds, but they correctly identified the solution imposed by the troika as 'medieval'. The troika, the sherpas, the nocturnal summits – this was a distortion of the community method of doing things, whose original aim was to create a new European economic and social policy, democratically discussed by governments meeting at the European council as well as by national and European parliamentarians.

AN ABSENT PROTAGONIST

We have arrived at a situation where the EU is being perceived more and more as a straitjacket on its member states, which is ironic if we consider its successes to date. Before this point of departure, the EU was considered a positive challenge. In Italy there was great mistrust in our political classes (just think back to the early 1990s and the era of political scandals and corruption known as *Tangentopoli*). Simply having an external point of reference that could indicate the right course and compensated for our national deficiencies was a relief to the electorate. In the 90s, the major Italian political parties, with a few minor exceptions, all espoused the European ideal with great conviction. Today the picture is quite different. European institutions are seen as a hindrance to implementing our own, different, national political will. To some extent, this is true, because some traditional EU policies are insufficient when faced with today's transnational challenges. Confidence in the union decreased, something that was predictable in view of the actions and mistakes of the last few years. Not only this, but also – and this, in my opinion is the more serious question we need to address – an indifference towards Europe has spread among its own citizens. Regaining lost trust is possible – and, as politicians, it is our duty – but how do we go about also involving citizens in, and exciting them once again about, all things European? To reference famous Italian author Alberto Moravia, 'the time of indifference' towards Europe is the greatest enemy we have to face.

However, there is a solution. It is not particularly original or imaginative, but, simply put, it is to bring politics back to the centre of Europe and Europe back into the centre of democracy. If we review the recent history of the EU, it becomes all the more evident that the issue is that we keep trying to offer the same solutions to different problems. Perhaps those solutions were in some memorandum of understanding filed under some incomprehensible name, as though there could be a one-size-fits-all solution to the crises we have experienced. Simple common sense should lead us to understand that there are too many variables to take into consideration, and what might work to solve one problem may not work in another situation. Within the EU, however, what happened was that, in parallel to the correct and justifiable exercise of national sovereignty, we imposed upon member states incorrect and unjustifiable technocratic controls and bureaucratic dominance from European institutions. The problem was never exercising sovereignty jointly with Brussels; it was ceding sovereignty to a bureaucracy that elevated technocrats in Brussels and those within national capitals to the level of Brahmins. These Brahmins most certainly celebrated the absence of the main protagonist in Europe – that of political direction.

If political direction has disappeared in the last few years it is because it has become subordinate to other players. The example often cited is the ambiguous – if not clearly subordinate – relationship between political direction and economic and fiscal policy that, in turn, has diminished the role of the state and left a free hand to market forces. It is certainly true that on many occasions the very subtle boundary between expansion of the markets and dominance of the markets was overstepped, as well as the boundary between the spread of neoliberal ideas and the sanctity of those same ideas.

That aside, regarding Europe, the problem is a different one. In addition to the 'Washington consensus', on this side of the Atlantic we also have to worry about the 'Brussels consensus' – a dangerous mix of fiscal conservatism and fear of inflation. The EU cannot be concerned only about budget evaluation or discussions on the output gap. That is not politics. That is accounting.

The result of all of this is a subtle, but constant, brainwashing by the preachers of fiscal conservatism. We were told, and it was plastered over the front pages of the newspapers, that we had to get used to living in an era of austerity, that would slowly heal our economic woes and deal with our debts. But this approach has only served to fuel the fires of social anger and popular frustration. It is the active negation of political action, because it does not accept that a political response is needed to face problems that do not stem from a balance sheet. I recall when, as a parliamentarian at the time, the first policy to counter the Greek problem was explained to us by senior members of the Italian government, the Barroso commission and the Bank of Italy. They delivered a detailed briefing on every minute detail, but not one word was uttered on the impact these measures would have on Greek citizens. When some of us questioned why the social impact had not been touched upon, the reply from our interlocutors left me dumbfounded: "We are not responsible for the social aspects."

We are now no longer willing to be held hostage by a policy of austerity. We want to turn over a new leaf and find a new path for Europe together: a path that should reflect a progressive vision for the future, one capable of finally overcoming the fences built around us during the years of the right's rule in Europe.

The problem is that the idea of Europe that was conceived not by our founding fathers but more by their founding children, has been blown off course by bureaucracy. Most of today's leaders are absolutely convinced that it is enough to hold 10 summits a year to solve the problems we are facing, even those delicate ones on the horizon. But the truth is that even if Mitterrand and Kohl were faced with these problems (and I have not seen any other leaders of their stature since) they too would not be able to put an end to the crisis in Europe. Gathering some 20-odd leaders in a room is not the way to deal with problems like saving the single currency. A Europe of managers, of admonition and of decisions already taken – which are only later placed on the table for discussion – cannot function. The problem is that little or nothing was done in the years preceding the crisis to resolve this ambiguity, with the result that when the storm arrived, we had no way of escaping from it.

If we already faced difficulties, misunderstandings and hesitancy when we were a union of 15 member states, imagine how these grew exponentially when we almost doubled in size. Throughout the euro crisis in particular, a series of questions resurfaced, which, despite the 20 or so summits held, did nothing to address the issues that divided and irritated the member states. On the contrary, everything was done to hide them under complicated formulae, because addressing them would have required a public debate, something that many leaders refused to hold. Europe needs to be built in a different manner, and to do so we must depart from the policy of crisis management and technocrats.

EMERGING FROM THE BUREAUCRATIC LABYRINTH

Very often in public debates, one country is singled out as the source of all our European woes: Germany. Without a doubt, Germany introduced reforms just when it needed to, ensured that its economy was competitive, and achieved hegemony in Europe. Hegemony, yes – but with little leadership and a lot of reluctance. There is no need for me to quote the vulgar and offensive headlines that appeared in some of our own daily newspapers to demonstrate how Europe, in the years of German dominance, has not functioned as effectively as it could or should have, and how it missed out on important opportunities and lost precious time.

This is in no way a criticism of the impressive progress achieved within Germany. However, I am less impressed by their actions at a European level, especially when Berlin keeps repeating that had every state done their homework, we would not have found ourselves in crisis. On this, Germany is off the mark, and by a long shot. Even if every member state had done its 'homework' (namely, structural reforms), the absence of eurozone governance would have still led to fundamental problems. Take the analogy of a city. If everyone's house was in order, but no one maintained the roads or the street lighting, and everybody refused to pay for common services, it would inevitably soon fall into decay. Weakening its common institutions, allowing the expansion of veto powers and becoming more bureaucratic, did not do Europe any good. Instead, it made it less immune to contagious diseases and lacking the resources to heal itself and get back on its feet after a crisis. Above all, this approach blurred Europe's identity. That said, Germany (who had several allies throughout this process) is not solely to blame, neither do I deny the responsibilities of those states who now find themselves in difficulty. However, Europe has lacked the ability to recover and to get back on track, as the United States, for example, was able to do. Europe is incomplete and it is not by reinforcing the powers of its capitals and weakening Brussels that we will get out of this predicament.

To paraphrase George Orwell, all European actors carry equal responsibility, but some responsibilities are more equal than others. I do not mean this as an accusation, it is simply the observation of someone who found himself seeing Europe from every angle: as a diplomat, at the European commission, in both the Italian and European parliaments, and from regional and central government. It is precisely because I believe in the European project and because I have dedicated so many years of my life to it – as a student, a university professor, a diplomat and a politician – that I feel bitter when examining the way things have turned out. Above all, during José Manuel Barroso's second term as president between 2009 and 2014, the commission completely refused to play its rightful role, instead becoming little more than a secretariat to the heads of state and government, always careful not to contradict them and taking every opportunity to appease the strongest among them. This is not the role that was intended for the commission within the European treaties and, above all, this is not the role that a key political actor like the commission should play. One may read and reread every single word of the treaties, but if the political will to interpret one's role as prescribed by the treaties is absent, there is really very little left to be done and the Berlaymont[1] is reduced to a cluster of offices.

The current president of the commission, Jean-Claude Juncker, thankfully, wishes to re-establish its relevance. On every occasion that Juncker has demonstrated this aim, he has had the full support of the Italian government. At the same time, Italy has not restrained its criticism each and every time that the Juncker commission has hesitated, backtracked or conceded to formalities and bureaucracy.

So how can we emerge out of the labyrinth? Not by continuing on the path of a minimalist Europe. It is wrong to think that the EU can live by European summits alone, with the obligatory 'family photo' of the leaders in attendance, or by a few sittings of the European parliament. If today the European institutions are perceived as empty shells, it is only because, during the course of the last few years, we have allowed them to be hollowed out. There are those who carry direct responsibility for this and others who did not do enough to prevent it, but together we allowed these institutions be filled with incomprehensible acronyms, dull formulae, and impersonal numbers, thus draining Europe of its political essence, its soul and its values. But a European Union without unity and without robust European values cannot – and should not – last. I recall a press conference given by an important socialist northern European leader who, throughout their answer to a question, did not stop quoting numbers and statistics. If this is Europe, it will not last long. As we see the first real political victory of the Eurosceptics in a leading European state, the very idea of European unity will again be placed in doubt, financial storms will once again pass over the most exposed states, and it won't take long until the few certainties we know today start to disintegrate. Is this really the story we wish to watch unfold over the next few years? I don't think so, but, if it is not, we need to move fast.

TACTICS VERSUS COURAGE

As I have already touched upon, in this entire debate there is one actor conspicuous in its absence – politics. Unfortunately, over the last few years this word has almost become a vulgarity – it has become a non-word that many hope will disappear from our daily lexicon. Let's be clear, those in the business of politics fed the anti-political mood. All too often politics seems incapable of offering effective solutions, of being conducted in incomprehensible language and accompanied by corruption and theft. But, notwithstanding any of this, I still cannot see how we can operate without politics.

It may be due to politics being a personal passion of mine, or that I have spent the last few years playing an active role as a parliamentarian, or because I cannot resign myself to the idea that we could go on without it. But if we are going to restart Europe in a complex international environment, overcoming the current practice of crisis management and returning to our original vision, then politics is the only means we have of achieving this.

Many difficult years precede us, when we found ourselves bitterly divided on important decisions. I can think of a number of recent historic crossroads for Europe that inflamed public opinion, and split political parties. As perhaps the most important example, take the enlargement of the EU towards the east in 2004. I recall that time very well because I had been working on it with Romano Prodi when he led the European commission. From its inception, the EU had been thought of as a continental project. After the fall of the Berlin Wall, history decided that we could not just stand by when confronted with the massive democratic transition that was taking place in eastern Europe. All of Europe, without exception, chose to lend a hand to help them along this chosen path. Were mistakes made during that process? Probably, but, then again, you can't make an omelette without breaking eggs.

The decision to expand the EU by admitting 10 more members was a political one, and there was a lot of uncertainty and doubt about it, but we all realised that we were standing at a momentous time in history and politicians knew that it was their responsibility to act. I ask myself what would have happened had we considered every voice that spoke out on the matter, had we weighed every single budget figure, each regulation comma. Without doubt, we would not have achieved the Europe we have today, albeit with all its contradictions and difficulties. However, I believe the process has not been completed, because enlargement was supposed to be accompanied by another important milestone, the adoption of a European constitution. That project failed after two unsuccessful referendums in founding member states: France and the Netherlands. This deprived a newly enlarged Europe of the political foundations that were absolutely necessary for the functioning of a united Europe. Eventually, many of the measures found in the constitution were implemented through the Lisbon treaty.

However, the French and Dutch referendums caused a certain loss of vision for Europe. The 'no' votes demonstrated fear, mistrust, and a loss of solidarity. The negative example from two founding states was unfortunately emulated in recent years by a declining perception of the EU and the election of Eurosceptic governments in a number of central and eastern European countries. Fear of the Polish plumber has been replaced by fear of the Syrian refugee.

There is great disillusion and irritation in some states towards others. I refer particularly to Poland and Hungary, who have even placed into question some of Europe's fundamental principles and rights, starting with the principle of solidarity. Just as surprising is the example of our British friends who pushed as hard as possible in favour of enlargement and then decided that their membership of the EU itself was up for discussion because, they claim, large numbers of eastern Europeans now live and work in their country. Make your mind up, guys.

Perhaps Britain's example is the best one to explain the biggest error that was committed – that of embarking upon such a historically ambitious project, which would reshape the future of Europe, without explaining to the European peoples the reasons behind it and all that was at stake. Yet another unfortunate example of short-sighted tactics over political courage. With officials too busy finding the right language to insert into the text of treaties, no attention was given to explaining to people what European enlargement would result in. We are all now aware of the result. European citizens did not spend their days reading the text of the constitutional treaty they were asked to vote upon. It contained too many complex articles, especially when compared to the alternative, leaner text presented by Prodi. People voted no because they felt that they were being asked to rubber stamp decisions that had already been taken, without the appropriate public debate and without being provided with the adequate information. All that was needed to defeat the project in France and the Netherlands was the unappealing image of a Polish plumber. The sad irony of this is that, with the current rate of economic growth in Poland, one would have to look hard to find a Polish plumber in western Europe nowadays. At the time, however, it was a very effective scare tactic as the EU had abandoned its responsibility to explain and defend its own political choices.

During the referendums on the treaty, there were populists on one side who urged voters to block a decision they claimed had already been 'taken', while, on the other side, there were those who wanted to implement a historic, but poorly explained, project. More ironic is the fact that Jacques Chirac only decided to call the referendum in France when it seemed almost certain that Tony Blair was about to do the same. The British referendum was never held, but France's took place in 2005 and went badly wrong. This is just one example, but I believe it is typical of what happens any time a decision taken by heads of government is put to their citizens without transparency, without debate and without democratic participation. These are mistakes that must not be repeated. It is at this stage that we must intervene. Our new policy for Europe must be one of reaffirming the supremacy of politics in Europe.

One must be clear, however, that emphasising politics does not simply mean reinforcing our institutions, it also means finding a new driving force and setting new common objectives, on which I will focus shortly. We must fill our empty boxes with men and women who are not only qualified but also filled with courage and strong political conviction. This is the biggest error of the last generation of pro-Europeans: thinking that politics could be subordinate to other issues. We currently find ourselves far away from the world in which the EU was established – an accomplishment that the former UN secretary general, Kofi Annan, later defined as the greatest political achievement of the 20th century. We find ourselves far from the spirit in which the first president of the European commission, the German Walter Hallstein, said that being *mutig* (courageous) was the most important quality required to be a real European leader. I think back to the building of Europe, which encouraged *tut etwas tapferes* (to conduct acts of courage). In recent years, however, we have seen very little courage in Brussels, Berlin or other European capitals.

THE ABSOLUTISM OF THE MARKET AND THE TECHNOCRATIC TOTEM OF CUTS ACROSS THE BOARD

For years we were sure that the best possible policy was laissez-faire. In the market, it went without saying: the more the state reduced its role, the better for the economy, which, in turn, would bring about benefits for everyone. I am a firm believer that the central idea upon which the EU was built (free movement of persons, as well as of goods, services and capital) is absolutely right. However, I also believe it is right and our duty to remember that, left unregulated, markets didn't solve their inefficiencies. Indeed, better state regulation would probably have helped avoid, and later remedy, the many market failures we have experienced.

I am convinced of the importance of a free market for the EU, but I am just as convinced that elevating the free market to the rank of an untouchable idol does no one any good, especially if strengthening it is done to the detriment of politics. In this regard the European right has a particular responsibility: pushing for a reduction in the role of the state in order to strengthen the market had the effect of radicalising the market ideology. But the left has just as much responsibility to bear. When the majority of governments in Europe and in the United States were progressive, they did not develop a political movement that could serve as an alternative to Ronald Reagan and Margaret Thatcher's neoliberalism. The difficulties most leftwing parties face today are, in part, a result of that fundamental error. When in government, the right did all it could to remove political and state action from the realm of economic policy. When progressives led some of the more powerful states in Europe, they were not able to develop a narrative for the European left that was just as strong and coherent. We experienced some domestic success implementing economic reforms, like those of Bill Clinton and Tony Blair in the 1990s and, to some extent, Gerhard Schröder. But all this did not really touch the EU. We missed a chance to implement a transnational reformist policy with the task of reforming Europe, rather than just taking place in Europe. Some countries did experience progressive reform, but a progressive way of governing was not reaffirmed at the continental scale, let alone on the world stage.

This is something we have been discussing for many years in the industrialised world. However we Europeans have managed to aggravate the economic crisis with the application of a recipe that was cooked up in Brussels with some German, Dutch and Finnish ingredients.

Austerity is a purely European creation, with a very clearly defined paternity – it was conservatives who brought it onto the European scene. The pattern is now well known: the right imposes a model, while progressives flounder and go off track. European socialists did not create this political imbalance, but – and we could hold a discussion on which was the worse mistake – they allowed it to take root in the corridors of Brussels until it became a dominant ideology. Austerity is not, as Alexis Tsipras has rightly said, found in any of the treaties (even to find mention of the eurogroup one needs to leaf through the various protocols of the treaties because, while it is very powerful, it is not a recognised institution). In a possible recipe on how to overcome the economic crisis it quickly became the yoke under which all European leaders at some point or other gave way, without much *mutig* but rather ill-advised and ill-informed by their throngs of technocrats and sherpas. Nonetheless, the worst consequence of this recipe was not economic but political.

The triumph of austerity allowed technocracy and bureaucracy to replace politics in the decision-making process. This is the legacy that the cultivators of this myth left us: the idea that the Brussels-based club with an excellent track record of implementing its rules and regulations and the application of a one-size-fits-all solution (even in the face of very diverse social and economic situations) could replace a popularly mandated executive and a democratic and transparent processes. To think that if we all did the same thing at the same time we would be able to achieve results beneficial for everyone is wrong because, when you're dealing with different national realities, we all have to do the right thing and what is right for one nation is not always right for another at that same point in time.

To take a concrete example: in general, the EU's decision to intervene to rescuing failing banks was a good one. The problem was that only one solution was found, the now infamous bail-in directive. However, the history, the management, and hence the problems of a Spanish bank are far different from those of an Italian, German or Dutch bank. Do we need common rules? Absolutely, yes. Do we need ideological totem? Absolutely not. In Italy, we dealt effectively with the crisis facing Banche Venete, Monte dei Paschi and other financial institutions facing difficulty. To do so, we worked closely with Margrethe Vestager, the best European commissioner responsible for this legislation.

For a number of years, Europe has been a laboratory within which to compress democratic dissent, with the conviction that anything that flows outside the strict parameters laid down by some Ecofin group in Brussels is automatically wrong and must be corrected. We can, alas we must, discuss the responsibilities of individual states – including Italy. But we cannot and must not forget that the strategy thought up by European conservatives, particularly those in the Nordic states, pushed us towards a Europe without politics – apolitical, rather than anti-political. This is a dangerous slippery slope, drifting in a direction that has little to do with democracy. As a result, if we do not react decisively today, with a change in politics and with more courage, we will find ourselves cornered in a terrible trap between technocracy and populism, from which we will all emerge defeated.

A RADICAL CHANGE OF PACE

Overcoming austerity. Sure, but how? And, above all, under whose leadership? The reply is as easy to say as it is difficult to implement. I am convinced that the problems we face in this period of European history can only be resolved if the reformist left can return to playing a key role in politics. The right cannot be our saviours, having contributed so much to weakening politics in every way over so many years – first by allowing an unregulated marked, then by enforcing technocracy to achieve a balanced budget.

Only a strong push forward by the progressive movement can provide the fuel needed to restart the European engine. We know the alternative all too well: that of resigning ourselves to the deadly technocratic-populist spiral and to our irrelevance on the global stage. The complexities of the age in which we are living are such that we cannot respond in a technical manner to challenges that are first and foremost political in nature. At the same time, globalisation imposes adjustments and disruptions on our member states to which solutions cannot always be found in our regulations and protocols. In other words, the solution is to return to the founding spirit of the original European project. The establishment of the EU and the creation of the euro were contemporaneous to an era of great transformation and globalisation. They were an attempt to anticipate and respond to the difficulties ahead. And yet, for some, it is all too tempting to believe that the euro and the EU are the cause of our current difficulties.

Today, Europe is cast in the role of villain, due to the many errors committed in recent years. It is true that its incomprehensible and complex way of doing business has supplied ammunition to its enemies. It is also very true that we need a better Europe, one that is more democratic and socially minded, more efficient and transparent. But, notwithstanding this, in the years to come, Europe is the only real resource our societies have to counter the huge global challenges we will face.

Constant attempts to divide the risks of the crises among member states rather than share them at EU level has noticeably weakened the effectiveness of economic and political action. However, it is vital that Europe's citizens understand one fundamental principal, whether they are German, Italian, or Greek, that greater European integration must be accompanied by an equivalent increase in information. Greater European solidarity must have a corresponding increase in responsibility by the individual states. If we remain trapped in a standoff between member states with little debt that are sceptical of those member states with high debt, and those states with structural weaknesses that place all the blame for their own failures on the EU, this crisis will drag on for decades.

We need a radical change of pace. We need to achieve our shared goals by voting on and ratifying the European treaties, not just those that refer to the public budget. In short, we need to strengthen the political union, which will, in turn, also serve to strengthen the European economy and glace it on par with other global giants, like the United States and China. To achieve this we need strong political structures, real economic solidarity and a commitment from each individual state to reform their legal, fiscal and labour regimes. Our economic development and the wellbeing of our people depend on this. If, however, we allow national selfishness to prevail, we will lose out on a historic opportunity, with only have ourselves to blame, because we will choose to succumb to fear rather than to prosper as a result of our courage.

The challenge facing our leaders is even more complex if we take into account the pitfalls that await us. We must be prepared to

stand up to those who are indifferent and to others who are professional demagogues. We must work with two goals: protecting our
idea of Europe, for which we have fought so hard over decades, and
also reforming Europe. The most serious mistake we could make
would be to believe the solutions of the past are enough to solve the
problems of the future. We cannot face our current economic and
social crises with the instruments we used 20 years ago. If the only
response we are able to muster is a vague draft of social democracy
2.0 then, frankly, it will be very difficult for us to rekindle the spirit
in the hearts of European citizens.

Instead, what we need is a left that is capable of moving beyond
the usual policies in order to succeed in a difficult task: that of stay-
ing true to its traditional mission while focusing on new objectives
and proposing them with new language. Some may ask if this is
possible, if delivering social justice with a new continental politics
is too difficult. But the alternative is to accept that the ills of our
societies are now irreversible, that we have to resign ourselves to a
world in which inequality is the rule not the exception.

Let's just think about the inequality of earnings. We have moved
from a disparity in earnings of 1:10 (which was considered acceptable following the 1929 crisis) to a ratio of 1:400 or more. We see
examples of a labourer's entire monthly wage falling below the
hourly salary of a manager in the same firm. In 2014, I found myself
in Amsterdam attending the Progressive Governance Conference.
There were many participants involved in progressive politics –
European social democrats, as well as American Democrats and
Canadian New Democrats. The conference examined the way in
which the economic crisis had impacted society. In many countries,
it is characterised by the formula '5-75-20' – five per cent being the
elite that hold most national and global wealth; 75 per cent being
the middle class (some of whom face growing difficulties and are
actually closer to the poverty line with little chance of real social
mobility); and finally the 20 per cent that are poor. This is the
snapshot of today's society, even in Europe, where we were all too
often convinced that the middle class was immune to the effects of

the crisis. We need new leadership and new domestic and European policies to promote growth, to strengthen the middle class and help those living in the bottom 20 per cent.

The question we face is simple: is politics still capable of addressing these issues or is it now akin to a decorative ornament, which we like to look at but is essentially of little use? Are we still capable of fighting for greater social justice, without rejecting the market economy? If we are, we need to prove it now. Otherwise, history will repeat itself and, once again, Europe will find itself unprepared. Almost a decade has passed since the onset of the crisis in 2008, when we found our institutions and our economic and social fabric ill-prepared for what lay ahead. Over the last ten years, Europe has moved much more slowly than the rest of the world. Therefore, what we must do now is adopt a completely different mentality. We need to change course.

A NEW LEXICON FOR EUROPE

When the Renzi government took office in February 2014, we had little choice but to roll up our sleeves and get to work. First of all, in Europe. The Italian presidency of Europe, which began in spring 2014, was fast-approaching. We set to work on a programme that was not about incremental change, but transforming our entire approach towards the EU.

I have already addressed what was not working within the EU. There is, though, a legitimate question: why Italy? Italy was, at the time, considered the sick man of Europe, second only to Greece in its financial woes (at least that's what one would have thought, hearing the not always very well-informed views of outside experts). Why did it fall to us to plant the flag of change in Brussels, fighting with all we had to establish a different model for development and economic growth?

As I suggested, after several months in my new role as under-secretary for European affairs in the prime minister's office, the answer was that Italy was able to find the right path out of this crisis. We admitted the mistakes we had made in the past (not undertaking the necessary reforms when the economy was growing, for example). We accepted the rules of the game (without missing any opportunity given to us to propose revisions) but we also put forward new objectives and a new language. We pushed for a different economic policy, the priority of which was to be growth, investment and employment. At the same time, we did not want anyone to doubt our seriousness. The time for out of control spending was over. Too many poor decisions in the past had left us with the terrible burden of a public debt that was also out of control. We wanted to change direction, but to do so responsibly: we could not continue to spend without regard for our children's future.

Furthermore, we wanted to change direction in other areas – with new programmes for the energy market and the digital agenda, as well as new policies for defending and protecting respect for the rule of law and human rights in Europe. We wanted a new language that would connect with Europe's citizens, which could break down the dubious certainties crafted by the conservatives and the austerity enthusiasts, and that would be capable of giving a lead in Europe to a reformed left. Above all, we said one thing very clearly: that the Europe we were faced with was too different to the continent described in the European treaties. It was a Europe fraught with double standards, which discouraged new ideas but allowed the implementation of policies proposed by those member states able to set the agenda and impose their priorities. It was not in our interest for Europe to be like this; Italy had suffered a lot in the last few years and, as Italians, we now needed to push as hard as we could to change things. The European status quo was not in our interest, and it was not the Europe we had promised, in treaty after treaty, to half a billion European citizens.

However, there wasn't a simple shopping list of things that needed to be done. We knew there was a mindset we had to overturn, so that is what we did. In rugby, when one faces the scrum, the referee always shouts 'engage!' And that is how we started. From day one, we used our ideas to free Europe from the deadlock it found itself in after years of inflexibility. The conservatives and the technocrats wanted to maintain that same deadlock. While we envisaged a new beginning, moving at high speed, others wanted to keep us on the equivalent of a slow-moving regional train. This was to be expected – we were just at the beginning of a political confrontation and it would have been a mistake of us to think that these inflexible positions would simply melt away on day one, like snow in the sun. But the debate was launched and battle commenced. We have already begun to see the first results and we must continue on this path.

Max Planck used to say that a new scientific truth does not triumph by convincing its opponents and making them see the light, but rather because its opponents eventually die out, and a new generation grows up that is familiar with it. Of course, nobody wishes death on the older generation, but we put our faith in the success of the fresh start detailed by Italy in our presidency programme and in the birth of a 'new European generation'.

In facing this challenge, words are important. Until 2014, no one in Europe spoke of flexibility, just to use one example. However, it was on precisely this word that we crossed swords with other member states. At the Ypres summit in June 2014, we spent the entire night negotiating a simple reference to that one word. Before that key meeting, some, even here in Italy, did not even want to utter the word flexibility, for fear of the reaction it would provoke. At Ypres, however, leaders spoke about it, making a commitment to use the 'flexibility' found in the Stability Pact and in other European regulations, in order to pursue the common goal of economic growth after stabilising our markets and our finances during the financial storm of the previous years. Flexibility is not a way to expunge the responsibilities of any one country. Neither is it a blank cheque from Brussels to its member states. It simply means that the application of any one rule without taking into consideration the context within which that rule is applied is not a regulation, but an ideology. It also means that the rules need to be applied intelligently, that is, in a way that encourages growth, reform and investment. We were first able to apply that flexibility to reward domestic reforms, then to encourage investment, to cope with the migration crises and, following the attacks in Paris, to allow for the special expenditure to enhance security in the fight against terror. These exceptions were not expected. They were part of a return to the primacy of politics (and, in some case, to the simple application of common sense) and the use of rules not as an end in itself but as a means to implement political choices and meet collective needs. We have finally opened up a crack. Now let's widen it, because we are just at the beginning, and there are still some attempting to close it shut.

Another example of the new European narrative is investment. This is a word that had become absent from the European conversation. Some were frightened to say it; others were simply indifferent. At the opening of a new session of the European parliament, Guy Verhofstadt, a great European, recalled the importance of the Delors plan as an example of how politics can be used to confront the problems that challenge us. A new policy for common investment, with fairer rules, including mobilising available financial resources and the development of new financial instruments, was proposed in particular by Italy and by the French government, led by François Hollande and Manuel Valls. It is on this basis that European governments and parliamentarians can and must work. We accepted and welcomed the 2014 Juncker Plan, but it is only the start. Brussels is mistaken if it thinks it can stem criticism of its failure to invest over the last few years, simply by redirecting a few billion euros, when much more is needed.

However, I want to look ahead with optimism. We have started to build the foundations of our new future. I only hope that we do not turn back and that we finally allow Europe to make the investments needed for successful energy, digital, transport, telecommunications, research and education policies.

But why do we consider public investment so important? Isn't private investment enough? I am fully aware of these objections. My answer is just as direct and clear: private investment is insufficient. It is certainly important, but if public investment does not play its part, we will never make the change that will enable the exponential growth across such a wide range of projects. I do not believe in the idea of a limited state, reduced to simply observing what is happening in the economic world around it. Neither do I have faith in an overweening state, which intervenes in every aspect of economic and industrial policy. Instead, to quote the title of Mariana Mazzucato's book, we need an 'entrepreneurial state'; capable of intervening where the private sector does not and, above all, helping to get the economy moving again. I was struck by an example used by Mazzucato: following Telecom Italia's privatisation in the 1990s, the first part of its budget to be cut was research and development. This demonstrates that, often, state action is not only welcome – it is also necessary. If we want to reshape the future, we should consider the package Barack Obama put in place to kickstart the American economy. The vast majority of its funds were aimed at infrastructure projects. Why? Because only the state can take certain decisions and run certain risks.

This is the challenge that Italy faces in Europe – rethinking the role of the EU and its member states, modernising it, making it both more substantial and more flexible. Mission impossible? On the contrary, it is the final chance for the country to stop living in the past and to lift its gaze towards the future. The goal of the governments of Matteo Renzi and Paolo Gentiloni was to approve crucial reforms for Italy, addressing deep-rooted problems. Can we reform the labour market? Can we build a civil service capable of using millions of bytes rather than tonnes of paper? Can we construct a democracy within which responsibilities, powers, and functions are clear and simple, allowing the government to govern in a manner appropriate for the 21st century, while also allowing those that wish to oppose it to do so in a legitimate manner? These questions confronted us at the start of 2014 when Renzi came to power. Have we achieved all our goals? No, and the failure of the constitutional referendum in December 2016 provides clear evidence of this. But when Renzi came to office in February 2014, the economy was mired in recession, contracting by 1.7 per cent. In comparison, in late 2017, the economy was growing by 1.5 per cent. During these three years, nearly 1 million jobs were created; exports increased by six per cent each year, with a positive effect on consumption and investment; and the number of women in the workforce reached its highest level for 40 years.

Revitalising Italy meant pursuing reforms that had been postponed for too long, or simply ignored because the status quo suited too many. In the past, many used the 'get out of jail free card': Europe made us do it. But we did not pass new labour and education laws because the Berlaymont wanted us to, and we will not confront every other challenge because we are on trial in front of a jury in Brussels.

Our message of a change in Italy is about demonstrating we are not schoolchildren who can be sent to the back of the class, but responsible adults who are fully aware of what needs to be done. We are undertaking reforms because we want change for ourselves and for our children. We are convinced that after decades of disasters, the Italian right has exhausted its ideas (so much so they now have to import them from Marine Le Pen) and we refuse to give up in the face of a few populist slogans – whether they hail from the Northern League or the Five Star Movement.

This is the prize at stake. A new generation has a great opportunity to get out on the field and play after sitting on the bench for far too long – but we don't have much time. Our country is back on its feet and now is the time to begin, without leaving anyone behind. Italy needs us to be reliable and credible – only by displaying these qualities will we be able to get our voice heard in Europe. After years of playing the 'sick man of Europe', Italy is being listened to and, in recent months, we have played a decisive role in dealing with some of the most complex issues Europe has had to face. So much so that those who once cast us as the 'sick man of Europe' are now asking themselves if we are becoming a European success story.

The deal Italy offers Europe is this: growth and employment is in everyone's interest. But if Europe approaches us in a spirit of distrust, pitting the northern European states against the south and vice versa, there will never be the necessary trust to build something new. This is why Rome approaches Brussels with this message: if policies for growth at a European level are not forthcoming, our reforms, even the most important ones, risk being ineffective. We are ready to commit ourselves to take all the necessary steps to relaunch the EU, but you, our European friends, are you ready to change direction?

NOTE

1. The Berlaymont building in Brussels is the seat of the European commission

THE CHALLENGE OF MIGRATION

I have often imagined 1950 as my parents and my grandparents described it to me through their stories: very few cars on the roads, high-waisted trousers, television shows that would arrive four years later in Italy, neorealism at the cinema and a country beginning to recover. However, during the 1950s, we also saw events that would forever change the course of European history. After 100 years of fighting each other literally to the death at more or less regular intervals, France and Germany launched a concept that would revolutionise, in a peaceful manner, relations between European states and peoples. We must begin with the words of Robert Schuman. While history is full of surprises, I like to think that nothing was left to chance. Schuman, then the French foreign minister, carried the symbol of a common destiny on his very own identity card. He was born in Luxembourg of a Luxembourger mother and a father from Lorraine: French by birth but German by citizenship and mother tongue. On the afternoon of 9 May 1950, Schuman read out a declaration in the Clock Room of the Quai D'Orsay that was destined to become the milestone for European integration.

AN INCLUSIVE WORD

Every time I have met with my former French colleague, Harlem Désir, at the Quay d'Orsay, I could not help but think about that day and the responsibilities we have today as European leaders, called upon to act in a period of change in our nations and the EU.

There is one key word in the declaration that is worth reflecting on. This word is 'solidarity': a word that is as crucial today as it was 65 years ago, a word that immediately embraces all those to whom it is directed, a word destined to include all that are excluded, and to restore a sense of nobility to our actions. "Europe will be built through concrete achievements which first create a de facto solidarity." This is at the heart of Europe, the heart of the path towards common integration, and the heart of the future of Europe, despite all those who oppose it. A concrete and tangible realisation for citizens to whom the memory of two devastating wars in less than 30 years was still all too alive.

Solidarity among member states, among European citizens, among the generations. Solidarity is the means through which we will arrive at a more inclusive Europe, one with a common identity that respects our differences and takes action to improve the lives of its citizens, by providing greater opportunity and new hope. We need concrete solidarity. Solidarity is not a new concept, but a value that has been present in Europe ever since this declaration that began its integration. This solidarity was put into action 65 years ago with the unification of industries as strategic and symbolic as coal and steel between two countries that had so recently fought two deadly wars but chose to make another conflict between them not only impractical but unimaginable.

The European leaders of the 1950s had the task of imagining a Europe that did not yet exist except in the dreams of a few. Today we have another duty: no longer imagining Europe but reforming Europe as it is in order to build the Europe that we wish to see. To achieve this, we need to defend the values for which Europe was created, fight for our rights and for the opportunities that only Europe can provide us, and confront with conviction and courage the debate on our common future. We must engage in dialogue, discuss, debate, explain, and defend the reasons for which Europe was created. We must reconsider rules and procedures that are inadequate in the face of current events. Rules and procedures are supposed to serve our fundamental values, our common objectives, and, above all, our political choices (and not vice versa). Those values are the advancement of solidarity, prosperity, social justice, security, defence, and our rights and social liberties in a rapidly changing world. To reaffirm the reasons we wish to remain united, we need to find new ways to explain what Europe has achieved over the last 65 years, as well as what it must become in the next 65 years and beyond. Today we must give value to that word – solidarity – as a fundamental principle sanctioned within our treaties and the basis of various common objectives that still need to be realised, from social cohesion to collective security and immigration.

OUR SOLIDARITY

Today we need to find our equivalent of coal and steel. When we do, we can launch our plan for solidarity, which should, above all, be political.

Today solidarity can be measured in a number of areas. If the EU wishes to continue, it must prove its solidarity in face of what Sergio Mattarella, the president of Italy, has termed the 'epochal emergency': the migration question.

We should recognise that it was not easy for the French and Germans to put aside the hatred they had cultivated over decades to act jointly in the name of solidarity. But their efforts allowed Europe as we know it to be born. We have a duty to create a different concept of solidarity – a solidarity of rights – starting with the realisation that the migration phenomenon can only be resolved together. Today we need to renew our approach, acting in greater harmony and more humanely when facing the crisis we are witnessing.

What is it we are witnessing? In an era of images, everything starts with an image. Scenes broadcast on the news, streamed on YouTube and shared on social media should make us understand the scale of the tragedy we face. We see images of migrant vessels, of migrant landings, of lifeless corpses engulfed by the Mediterranean. Seeing these, I often could not suppress my feelings of anger and frustration. Anger because all too often we have said 'never again', only to witness such tragedies repeat themselves. Frustration because I cannot, and do not want to think, that Europe is impotent to act when faced with thousands of deaths.

We see images of refugees arriving at a Berlin train station wrapped in a blue flag adorned with 12 gold stars, having escaped the Islamist extremists who decapitate people in cities they have taken over, like Sirte, and massacre young people in Europe at venues like the Bataclan. Our shame is the tiny corpse of Alan Kurdi – a child of just three who perished and washed ashore on a Turkish beach – alongside the other children escaping murderous extremists who die anonymously at sea.

These two images have been at the front of my mind in recent months, each time we have discussed the issue of migration in Rome or in Brussels. They are, however, also the images which give me the strength to persevere because only through concerted European action can we tackle the issue of immigration. If we act alone we will not only see continued migration, but also the cheap demagoguery of the likes of Marine Le Pen and Matteo Salvini who exploit these tragedies without offering any viable solutions. They exploit our fear and gamble with our lives and our freedoms. We cannot allow them to do this. We Europeans have already paid too high a price to nationalism and populism.

Who are those thousands who have perished? First and foremost, they are human lives that have been lost. People who have cruelly drowned, simply because they harboured a desire to rekindle their hopes – or, more often, simply to survive – away from their countries of origin. They are forced to do so out of pure desperation – the result of hunger and war. I think we all need to make an effort to consider why these migrants undertake this voyage, why they risk drowning on a rickety boat in the Mediterranean. The answer is very simple. We are the answer. It is us they yearn for. Europe: a western society based on equal rights and freedoms, on equality and hospitality. The migrants who raise their gazes from Libyan shores towards Europe are, in reality, looking at us. At what we are. At what we have become. It is in reaction to these same freedoms – but with the opposite attitude to the refugees and economic migrants – that Islamist terrorists wish to destroy us.

The history of Europe is one of people who took to the seas to discover new horizons, both within and outside the known world. It is the sea that guided Ulysses in his voyage to Ithaca – a founding myth of a European community that made movement of people its reason for being. This is why we cannot accept tragedies like those occurring off the coast of Lampedusa. We cannot let the Mediterranean – the sea of Europe – become its 'dead sea', a cemetery of selfishness, European indifference and the absence of action.

No, Europe cannot look away. Our history, our values and our future are at stake. Europe must deploy all its humanity and confront this situation. Those who have drowned in the Mediterranean are European victims. We have an absolute duty to find a twin solution – to how we receive and integrate new migrants and solve the instability of the Mediterranean region. If Europe does not step up to manage new influxes of migrants, it will inevitably suffer and be overwhelmed. There is a good lesson from history: the fall of the Roman empire began when Rome closed its doors, stopped integration and discouraged people from different cultures living together.

The alternative path is one taken by a society that chooses not to care about this tragedy, who does not act and ignores the dead, as if there were two classes of human being – one worth more than the other.

Those who think in this way should have the courage to say so out loud, without hiding behind a façade of concern, or behind cynical political and electoral calculations. At primary school, my generation studied several authors and poets who witnessed with their own eyes and who made us relive through their writings the tragedies of the second world war and the displaced people it created. Writers like Primo Levi, Giuseppe Ungaretti, Jacques Prévert and Eugenio Montale, who in his poem 'Perhaps One Morning Walking' wrote: "But it will be too late, and I will return silently, to men who do not look back, with my secret". We must not be 'too late'. We must not be people who do not care about others, who think only of protecting ourselves, turning away from what is happening in the world around us. We must show the courage of solidarity and adopt a more far-sighted new policy for the Mediterranean.

It requires courage because, if we are afraid, we cannot have solidarity. Unfortunately, Europe in the last few years has seemed more like a theatre of fear than of hope. But how much fear must we face until we respond by looking our future squarely in the face? The 9/11 attacks brought the fear of terrorism, realised through the attacks in London and Madrid. This preceded a fear of our fellow Europeans, fear of them taking our jobs. And finally we had the fear of migrants. This fear has conditioned our way of life, our way of acting as a society, our way of doing politics. We imprisoned ourselves within our own fears, surrounded by invisible walls of selfishness. The same walls we tore down in order to create our Europe – those hateful walls surrounding Auschwitz; that wall that divided Berlin, separating eastern and western Europe for decades – have reappeared as new wounds on our continent. These new walls, whether made of cement, such as that between Hungary and Serbia, or merely forged from selfishness and hypocrisy, like the barrier between Calais and Dover, weaken our politics and shame our values. We will remember 2015 as a year of tragedy, for Charlie Hebdo, for the deaths on the Mediterranean seabed, for our young people murdered on that cursed 13 November in Paris. There are those who want to respond to this by building a wall, as though a pile of bricks some four or five meters high could be the panacea for all the ailments found in our society: a society unable to solve its afflictions without resorting to barbed wire. Our Europe was born from the destruction of the walls of Auschwitz. It fought for 40 years to demolish the Berlin Wall.

It cannot stand idly by and witness the construction of other walls. In 2014, I celebrated the 25th anniversary of the fall of the Berlin Wall, alongside Michael Roth, the German minister for European affairs, and other colleagues in the city where Michael was born and raised: Heringen, in Hesse, a few kilometres from the wall. Michael was raised in a home across the road from the wall, on the European and democratic side. On our visit, we planted seven trees, one for each of our countries, to symbolise the unity of Europe, next to trees that grew during the years that the wall divided Europe into two.

Our generation grew up with the wall. We remember all too well what it means to divide peoples and states with force and violence, and that those who build walls inevitably become prisoners of the closed societies they construct.

Whenever I listen to the latest populist or racist attacking migrants on TV – sometimes to the extent of advocating the turning back of their vessels – I feel they are besmirching our values. They suggest we leave the fate of these people to the sea, trying to make us believe every Syrian refugee is a possible killer. When I hear them, I feel that I am not listening to the erroneous views of an individual, but witnessing a collective failure. We have allowed a strain of racism to contaminate our society without taking the necessary vaccinations. Thus, we find ourselves with a nationalist in government in Hungary, with an extreme rightwing party through to the recent presidential runoff in France, with the xenophobic right becoming the second most popular party in Denmark, and with the ultranationalists in government in Poland. We again find ourselves in a Europe being corroded from the inside by neo-Nazi nationalists and from within and without by Islamist extremists. Yes, Europe is today under attack – but it is not a conflict among states, it is an attack by barbarians against our civilisation. And we are not taking into account the domino effect that this has created. Under pressure from extremist forces, governments have adopted more hardline positions. If someone had suggested abolishing Schengen 10 years ago, they would have been taken for a mad man. However, today many are suggesting this as a possible solution.

BETWEEN FREEDOM AND SECURITY

It is always the demagogues of the day who promote the most deceptive solutions. Shutting down Schengen means undermining our liberties. And if we were to do so, it would hand barbaric terrorists their greatest victory and would in no way enhance our security. The aim should not be to abolish our freedoms under Schengen but to make better use of them by building real common European borders and a real integration of European police forces. It is unthinkable that sole responsibility for the issue of migration should rest with the states where the migrants first arrive. Insisting on this approach strains the very fabric of Europe – and it is the approach taken by those who think only of themselves; after all, how many asylum seekers arrive in Slovakia or Poland? It is unsustainable, as it requires us to define Lampedusa as more (or less) European than Helsinki, or Hamburg, which receives thousands of migrants each month, more (or less) European than Bratislava. Things cannot work this way.

If we lack solidarity when faced with such challenges, organising council meetings or summits is pointless. If the EU does not accept the fact that its role is to act fast, we risk facing two challenges. The first is the one we see on the news: our incapacity to manage the migratory flows, refusing to take any leadership role in the Mediterranean, the tired resignation with which we shrug when faced with these continuous tragedies. The second is more risky and dangerous in the long term: failing to provide a solution to the xenophobia coursing through the veins of our society.

A Europe that gives up in the face of the migration crisis, abandoning its own member states to handle unsustainable situations (I think especially of Italy and Greece, forced to absorb the full burden of hosting tens of thousands of refugees), raises a white flag in the face of populism. The real paradox, if we think that only the EU can provide the strength and resources to deal with this phenomenon, is that some states propose to effectively destroy the union rather than build the Europe we need. We cannot return to the days when nationalism led European citizens to massacre each other in extermination camps, or that led the continent to be divided between east and west for over 30 years. The Balkan wars, the ethnic cleansing, the tragedies we saw in Srebrenica should remind us of the violence Europeans are capable of in the absence of unity. Let us not forget that, even when the Europe we know today was starting to take shape, far-right dictators ruled countries like Spain, Portugal and Greece.

Ukip, the Northern League, the National Front, Jobbik and other variations of European hatred have shown that if we do not stop this spiral, the very survival of our democracy will be at risk. If we succumb to short-sightedness, weakness, fear, and populism, we will see our borders come down once again, protectionism will reign on either side of the Rhine and the Alps, and nationalist violence will be rekindled. We cannot allow our values to be shot down by the nationalist snipers.

Serbian snipers destroyed the lives and futures of many innocent people in Sarajevo. I remember the city during the war. As a young diplomat, I was involved with the embargo against Serbia. I remember 'Sniper Alley' well – a long corridor connecting the airport to the city, through which one had to race at 130km/h in order to avoid the snipers' bullets. I also recall just as well the time I spent in Sarajevo during its reconstruction. I had never seen so many wheelchair-bound young people, so many open wounds. Most young people did not want to speak about the war. Neither did I. They only wanted to talk about their future, a future in which they saw just one thing – Europe. It is these experiences that forged my European beliefs.

THAT ORANGE LIFE JACKET

In 2016, those same parts of the Balkans are once again in crisis due to the migratory flows we are experiencing. This is yet another reason why we must not fail: this time we have an appointment with history.

Does another solution to all of this exist? Nothing is ever simple. It is infinitely easier to say 'away with the immigrants' than to stop and think how we can guarantee a better life for those already in our societies as well as to those desperate people, together. But everything would be easier if Europe decided to transform its civil strength into action.

It took all those deaths at sea to finally move Europe into action. After many months of work, the first glimmer of solidarity appeared. Following the extraordinary European council held at the end of April 2015, we finally reached an agreement on the redistribution of asylum seekers during the crisis. It was then discussed again (until three in the morning) at the summit held at the end of June. The resulting agreement was fair. It recognised that Europe must deal with up to 160,000 asylum seekers through a reallocation mechanism. Finally, through this concrete and operative mechanism, the EU has started to assume its responsibilities. The package of measures the EU adopted represent a first step in the right direction. However, we have seen a deliberately slow implementation of this fair and just agreement, with many problems raised and much resistance shown by some member states towards respecting the commitments made in the name of solidarity. No, dear colleagues in European governments, we are not yet where we ought to be; some of you are still not showing that you understand all that is at stake here.

I accept all the objections that boil down to, how can one talk of a common path when many member states don't do anything but put down caveats, and invoke opt-outs? I'll admit that I had hoped for a bigger uptake from other member states. But we must not give up. We must not be discouraged. We have started down a real path of solidarity, and this is an important development. Only a few years ago it would have been impossible to imagine talking about solidarity, responsibility sharing and a new European migration policy.

Now that the battle over the principle has been won, it is essential that all those who have agreed to it respect the commitments they have made, because we are in the midst of a difficult situation, and we cannot play politics with people's lives.

On this issue, we cannot retreat. Solidarity cannot be a one-way street. It cannot exist only when we hand out development funds to eastern European countries. Everyone must respect the rule of law and human rights, in particular the right of asylum and immigration obligations, as stressed by European leaders in the Rome declaration, signed on 25 March 2017. We are pleased that the Renzi government's proposal to link the release of EU funds to member states' respect for the rule of law was recently taken up by commissioners Günther Oettinger and Corina Crețu, and emphasised by Martin Schulz, in his election campaign in Germany. We should not give funding to those who do not uphold the rule of law, starting with the welcoming the redistribution of migrants. The EU's credibility among its citizens is tied to its protection of human rights. One cannot be pro-European when it is time to cash in, but nationalist when it is time for solidarity and respect for fellow citizens' rights.

From all of this we have learned two lessons, one for Europe and the other for Italy.

In Brussels, they have finally realised that a problem that risked being insurmountable for one country alone, can be better dealt with and – hopefully – resolved if managed collectively. After all, isn't this the mission of the European Union? Why can we not imagine that our common efforts on immigration could lead to a renewed idea of integration? In our history, in Europe's history, there is no place for closed borders.

The second lesson is for Italy. The dramatic migration crisis showed another side to our country, as no longer a country that creates problems, but one that solves them. No longer the country that cannot achieve anything without Europe, but the country that showed Europe how to act in such circumstances. Faced with capsized boats off the coast of Lampedusa, we sought assistance from Europe, but in the meantime we rolled up our sleeves, first launching Operation Mare Nostrum and then, with the inclusion of other nations, transforming it into a joint European operation, Triton. Our naval personnel displayed true courage, and it is on the strength of this that we can look our European colleagues squarely in the eyes, convinced that if

Europe wishes to play a role in the world, it must demonstrate that it is capable of doing so in the Mediterranean, starting with Libya.

On my office desk, I keep a discoloured orange life jacket, covered in writing, given to me by Guul Isha of Médecins Sans Frontières. She is a young Somali woman, who was persecuted for her political beliefs, risked her life on a rickety boat and survived the crossing thanks to our navy and the NGOs that worked with us. On that life jacket, she wrote vital information, including telephone numbers of who to contact in case her attempt failed, and a poem – a hymn to life and to hope. Every time foreign delegations enter my office, it is the first item they notice. That is what our country is all about. And we would like Europe to become like this too.

WHAT THE LEFT HAS NOT SAID

The topic of migration is close to my heart because I feel that it is the real test for the European left if it wishes to face up to the challenges of government. Immigration naturally encompasses multiple issues: how we treat new arrivals, challenges around illegal immigration, how we improve integration. It is a decisive issue, if not *the* decisive, issue, that, together with the economy and security, will define us. Are we able to speak to a housewife in Voghera, but also to a white-collar employee in Cesena or to a labourer in Catanzaro? To voters who feel security is their priority and thus may be afraid to vote for the left, might we be able to persuade them if they felt our candidate offered a better solution on this issue? This may seem a problem specific to Italy, but it is the same challenge faced by Labour in Britain, the socialists in France and the SPD in Germany.

We need to be clear when we talk about migration. We must take into consideration the human aspect of the phenomenon, not the emotional one; there is a big difference between the two. If we get used to thinking of migrants simply as numbers (how many arrive, how many leave, how many die) we will never be able to understand the enormity of the situation. Our challenge is to confront the situation rationally. We cannot listen to only our gut feeling. We must use both our hearts and our heads.

First, we must consider the case of asylum seekers. These people can no longer remain in their countries of origin because of their religion, political opinions or other beliefs. These people are escaping almost certain death: their government has become a threat to their very existence. It is not a good heart but a sense of justice that leads us to assist them. It concerns a universal human right that Europe cannot ignore. We cannot have a ceiling on the numbers of migrants who may attain asylum in Europe. We must welcome all those whose asylum status has been legally recognised. This is where Europe comes into play and we have to revise the principles of the Dublin treaty: that each asylum request must be examined by the state that played the most significant role in the individual's first arrival in the EU. Asylum seekers are looking for a European asylum – not one that is specifically Italian, German or Greek.

We must define in a clear – and European – manner the necessary criteria to meet a request for asylum, and harmonise our procedures to do so. People should not have to wait two years.

At the same time, if reception is dealt with at the European level, then the management of repatriation procedures also has to be. It is unacceptable that reception, identification and repatriation is the responsibly of only some states. This is an abrogation of the principle of European solidarity. The truth is that when we speak about people who are running away from war, men and women who risk everything for the possibility of a better future, we are talking about ourselves. Let's think about it for a moment. If Italy were struck by just one of the afflictions faced by the people of Africa or the Middle East, would we not want our neighbouring countries to receive us and to offer us new hope? This is how it worked in the past for those who left their homes in the hope of finding opportunities that were not available to them in Italy at the time. This may no longer be the case today, but who can guarantee that we will not find ourselves again in that situation in the future, perhaps because of climate change?

Unfortunately, we do not uniformly have the spirit of hospitality running through our veins in Europe. I am talking about all those who, overwhelmed by the fear and irritation of having to deal with new cultural, ethnic and religious differences, want to live in a past that no longer exists.

But this is not the world we want. This is not the world that we are fighting for. Our civilisation is founded on the principle that people should have equal opportunities and be able to distinguish themselves by their diverse abilities. We should ask honestly if all European citizens share this vision, or whether fear towards those trying to reach our shores as they try to escape the terrors of war are, sadly, becoming stronger. I remain convinced that our values commit us to recognise these refugees as our brothers and sisters, who are escaping mortal danger. Yet, all too often, people do not want them here and emphasis the problems they create for us, ignoring the many advantages we derive from their presence. We call for heavy penalties against foreigners who break our laws but remain silent against Italians that may commit the same crimes. In the Italian parliament, for example, there are those who call for a tough sentence against a Romany who ran over pedestrians standing at a traffic light while, at the same time, pushing amendments to allow more lenient sentences for those found guilty of committing crimes while drunk driving.

It is time for a great truth-revealing operation, without which any attempt to tackle the issue of migration will be in vain. We need to clear the air of the lies, allegations, and half-truths that surround this topic. About a year ago, I was struck by the results of an Ipsos Mori poll that highlighted the level of ignorance in various member states. The 'index of ignorance' was defined as the difference between the perception of a phenomenon and the reality. This difference is reduced if respondents are well informed. Those who are uninformed and base their opinions solely on hearsay, have less access to facts and their measure of ignorance increases. When asked the level of migrants in their country, Italians suggested 30 per cent, Belgians 29 per cent and the French 28 per cent. True of False? Absolutely false. Immigrants constitute just seven per cent of Italy's population, while the level in Belgium and France is 10 per cent. The majority of Europeans have a distorted perception of reality. They believe that they have been besieged by migrants, that they are a species heading towards extinction, but this is simply not the case. The situation is naturally a complex one, but the perceived 'invasion' of migrants does not existent.

We have to face reality. This goes both for those who play on our fears as well as those who appeal to our altruism. We need to come up with concrete, pragmatic solutions that balance saving lives and receiving migrants with guaranteeing European security. Repatriating those who do not have the right to reside here is a vital part of the solution. This action is neither immediate nor easy as, to achieve this, we need to engage in a dialogue with the countries of origin and reinforce our co-operation with them, as well as utilise new resources. However, it is a necessary part of the solution – just as necessary as allowing legal migration, ensuring economic and social integration, providing a welcome to those escaping wars and persecution, and fighting against illegal people trafficking and organised crime.

In Italy, the Northern League has exploited xenophobia for years, even when, as part of Silvio Berlusconi's governing coalition, it held the interior minister portfolio. In reality, when it was in government, the Northern League did very little to address the issue of security. And the little it did, it did badly. During its tenure, it cut the budgets allocated to the various security agencies in Italy and introduced the biggest measure in the last 30 years to regularise the position of illegal migrants. It also signed the Dublin treaty and, in doing so, implied Italy take charge of a disproportionate number of asylum procedures as country of first arrival – as oppose to push for a fair sharing arrangement. This is proof that they do not even believe in what they preach as, once in power, they did exactly the opposite of what they had advocated. Almost a million of the 'hated' migrants, as Northern League leader Matteo Salvini described them, were regularised by the party in government. Perhaps because even they realised that in Lombardy, one of the most developed regions in Europe, it would be impossible to take care of the elderly without migrant workers. In Lombardy, there are 130,000 people working in the care sector, 95 per cent of whom are foreigners. There is no better example with which to imagine what Italian, and European, society would look like without the constant influx of migrant workers, not to mention the valuable input of migrant labour for industry. We should also be aware that in an ageing society this is a phenomenon destined to grow, not shrink.

However, talking about the incompetency of our political opponents will not win us votes. It is not enough for us to point out that they achieved very little in government – even though this may be true – we also have to highlight what we want to achieve. We need to sing from a new hymn sheet. Repeating the same mantra of reception and hospitality is no longer sufficient and, frankly, I do not believe that it is possible to welcome every person who wishes to move to Europe to improve their economic status. We need the courage to say that we have to find a common system with which to manage economic migrants. We must set out credible proposals for debate – perhaps that advanced by Guy Verhofstadt to introduce an annual European quota on economic migrants and provide a 'blue card' granting them the right to enter the EU, similar to the American system.

First, we should facilitate family reunification. If a person lives and works in Europe, we should enable their family to join them. Then there are entire sections of our economies that require migrant workers. We should facilitate this in an intelligent manner. At the same time, we cannot absorb all those who arrive without distinguishing among them, because we must be able to guarantee a decent life for these migrants as well as ensure their integration into our society. The former French prime minister, Michel Rocard, was right when he declared: 'we cannot welcome all the misery of the world.' Nevertheless, we must do more to tackle that misery.

We should fight for certain rights to be recognised, but insist that those who enter our countries agree to respect certain duties and obligations. Here lies the heart of the question – where even the most clear-sighted policies have been, sometimes, at fault: guilty of failing to provide clear rules that establish how and why a migrant may become an Italian and European citizen.

I want to be clear in my words, to ensure they are understood. I believe we must not limit ourselves to receiving migrants, and providing them with food and assistance. However, we cannot we afford to turn them into Italian citizens without their understanding the society that they live in. We must welcome migrants because it is right and because it is in our interest to do so, but we also need to do more to transform them into citizens who aware of their rights as well as their obligations.

In response to those who disagree, I believe it is unacceptable that a person who believes he is ready to become an Italian citizen be accompanied by a retinue of women that he considers an inferior species or think religious difference constitutes a mortal sin. We must help those we welcome to become Italian and European citizens, but we must also win them over to our values. Among these are, above all, our constitutions and the European charter of charter of fundamental rights. These should always come first – even before, for example, the Qur'an or the Bible.

In the United States, new citizens take an oath of allegiance to the American constitution. I feel that this is absolutely right. If you embrace a country, then you also embrace its highest values. In the case of Italy and Europe, these values relate to individual liberties: the freedom to believe or not believe (and to satirise those who do); democracy; equality of the sexes; the prohibition of discrimination based on race, gender or religion; the right to exercise political free will. New arrivals must accept that certain things that are prohibited in their country of origin are perfectly legal here. In our societies, women are free to choose what they wear, whom they wish to marry, what to study and where to work. An understanding of the language of the country where the migrant wishes to work is also indispensable.

This is what we have to ask of the migrants we receive – the recognition of our values in exchange for the recognition of their needs.

Tackling this alone will present countries with growing difficulties, but working together, through European institutions, provides the means, the resources and the opportunity to better overcome these challenges. This is exactly where our efforts are directed. We intend to 'Europeanise' the problem. An Italian solution to the immigration situation does not exist; neither does a Greek, Spanish or German one. But there could be a European solution. Europeanising immigration means accepting compromises but also standing firm on certain points: on repatriation, procedures for identification, and the fight against traffickers. What has been missing in Europe, and what, in my opinion, we still need to achieve, is a holistic strategy on migration. A realistic strategy, but one that is also true to the values that inspired the creation of our union. It would require more courage, and more knowledge of geography: the southern borders of Europe would be the fulcrum of the entire policy.

This year, which has seen increasing numbers of arrivals on the Italian coast, has reminded us that the issue of migration is crucial for the future of the EU. Any thought of leaving Italy to its fate in this moment, when our ability to manage the reception of migrants has reached its limit, means surrendering to short-sightedness and self-interest. It means accepting that, in the face of big challenges, the EU becomes small, finding its authority only when new regulations and budgets are at stake.

Personally, I think the EU deserves better than that. Jean-Claude Juncker ended his speech in front of the European parliament in July with the words 'viva l'Italia'. This message has been echoed at the most recent European summits. No European leader has advocated leaving Italy to its fate.

Now it is time to move from words to deeds. Italy has proposed a brave and practical plan to manage immigration, which has won an almost unanimous consensus. Some important points include facing the issue in Libya, drafting a code of conduct for NGOs and reinforcing return procedures.

Libya is our number one priority. We must increase the funds already made available by the commission. The disparity between the means given to Turkey to close the Balkan route and those given to Libya to control African flows is not acceptable. What would those new funds be for? They could reinforce the Libyan coastguard to control its territorial waters, increase the presence of the International Maritime Organisation and the UN refugee agency, and reinforce Libya's southern frontiers, which represent the real European border with respect to the issue of migrants. We cannot delay the establishment of UN welcome centres in Libya.

Lastly, return policies are of fundamental importance. We have been pushing for a European visa policy. Those countries that do not allow repatriations will be subject to restrictions on their visas.

In the face of a migration emergency, Italy proves its commitment every day. We are asking Europe to act as a continent, and to have the necessary ambition to govern a regional phenomenon, which cannot be left in the hands of a single country.

If Europe continues to fail to rise to this challenge, if it cannot marry the protection of rights and the need for security, it will wither away until it becomes, in the words of Radiohead in High and Dry, 'the one who cannot talk'.

THE MOTHER OF ALL QUESTIONS

If you perform a Google search for the word 'Europe', the first result will most probably be the Europa League. As a passionate football fan, I understand this. If you google 'Europa League' you get almost 74m results. You get less than half this if you change the search to 'Europe crises' (just over 31m). Google 'Europe immigration' and you get a tenth of this – just over 6m results. If that does not satisfy you, search for 'Europe demography' and you get a mere 809,000 results, just over one per cent of the search results for 'Europa League'.

Why is no one talking about demographics? In my opinion, it is the great issue upon which all of our policies must be based in the coming years. Demographics intertwine with so many crucial aspects of our society: from the economy to welfare, from education to immigration. Every available indicator shows Europe is a continent with an ageing population. We find this not only in eastern Europe, where the fertility rate is in constant decline – of all the 28 member states, only France and Ireland rank above the EU average of two children per family. According to the available statistics, central and eastern Europe are getting ever older. A few years ago, the World Bank published a study discussing politics and demography, which was provocatively but accurately entitled, 'From Red to

Gray'. The reality is this: how does a country like Poland, which in 2050 will have a population of 32 million – the same level as today – envisage its future? At that point, one Pole in two will be aged 65 or over, a drastic drop in the working age population. The trend is very clear, especially if we consider that, on average, European citizens are living longer, thanks to welfare systems that are, without a doubt, the best in the world.

THE RISK OF A BLOCKED SOCIETY

These are alarming statistics, so it would be a good idea to discuss them and study them, so we are prepared to take important social policy decisions to tackle the situation. Instead, no one – or almost no one – is talking about it.

An ageing population is one that does not look at its future through the same lens. Italy would be a good case study. We are having fewer children, and this has an impact beyond the statistics. Let's look at just this one. In Italy, thanks to the 'only child generation' we find five million people aged 45 to 49 years old, while there are just three million between the ages of 20 and 24. This means that there are 2.5 million fewer young people today than there were 25 years ago. The consequences such a drop is not only a more elderly population, but also a radical change in society. An ageing population produces fewer families and is less active in the labour market. This has been dubbed the 'crisis in the crib' that, over the medium to long term, could translate into a fiscal crisis (as the state will be able to collect far less tax over time) and cause problems for the economy as we have fewer consumers and a smaller labour force. The greatest risk we run is of being confronted with a 'blocked society', a term originally coined by French sociologist Michel Crozier in the 1970s. Such a population is less like to experiment and innovate and more inclined to save and become more conservative.

How much could all this cost us? The low fertility rate is just one of the problems and raising the retirement age only compensates slightly for this, as its growth is too slow. The consequences are alarming as the estimated cost of such a diminishing active population is as much as half a percentage point per year in GDP growth.

Are policymakers taking this into consideration? When we say society is changing, we must talk not just of digitisation but – above all – the composition of our societies.

Fortunately, we have two important opportunities to remedy this: family and youth policies, and migration policy. In particular, through an effective management of the migration phenomenon, Europe has the chance to invert the demographic crisis and transform itself from a land of emigrants to one of immigrants. However, in order to achieve this, we must do what we have so far been unable – or unwilling – to do: tackle the issue of migration, as suggested in the preceding chapter, and create new opportunities for our young people, as we are doing in Italy through reforms to employment law, schools and the national curriculum. We can and must devise the necessary national solutions through serious reforms in those areas that are critical to our future.

To truly tackle the phenomenon we must nevertheless develop a transnational policy, and the EU is the only means to achieve this. We need to confront not only the tradition left and right. In the last few years, new actors have entered the scene – the populists. Initially confined to minor roles, they have become more and more central to the political and social debate.

Looking back now, the Dutch Pym Fortuyn movement seems to belong to a different era. Over recent years, populist political forces have managed to insert themselves into the folds of society; now they run local councils, have attained seats in parliaments, and are in pole position for upcoming elections – all reinforced by the technocratic path chosen by the EU.

How has this happened? Populist tensions are inherent in every society. It is just that, for a long time, we were under the illusion that we had suppressed them; the left and right confronted them and removed seemingly rid themselves of many of these instincts. This was possible as politics continued to turn on a left-right axis and while

European societies were not subject to great changes. However, over time, our certainties began to disappear and European society began to change. Standards of living improved, we chose to have fewer children, we grew older and levels of inward migration increased.

We should consider this one piece of data: Eurostat research shows that Germany and Italy are respectively the first and fourth largest European countries by population, and they owe their demographic growth solely to immigration. France and Britain – respectively, the second and third largest EU member states – are maintaining their position thanks to higher birth rates.

Whether we like it or not, we depend on migrants. Of course, we can make pretend this is not the case and carry on as before. In 2007, Gordon Brown, the then Labour prime minister, used the phrase 'British jobs for British workers' – a nonsense slogan that was a display of political weakness.

Responsible political forces should start at the place that has no political colour: reality. Choosing the path of reality would lead us to welcome refugees arriving in Europe – not for charitable but pragmatic reasons. In fact, it is estimated that, despite the huge increase in public expenditure needed to manage the migratory crisis, in the medium to long term – let's say within 10 years – these migrants will contribute substantially to sustaining our pensions. In short, there are many good reasons to implement a policy of reception and integration at the European level, given problem is common to all (or almost all) member states, and not just of a few.

Instead, we have to face populists – from left and right – who pretend they can solve the problem by flying in the face of reality. In 2015, Europe experienced a larger death rate than birth rate. We must immediately confront this or we will end up like Japan who, if they do not invert their demographic trends, risk their population shrinking by 41 million in 48 years. As a study by the Japanese health ministry suggests, at the current pace, the population will fall by two thirds within a century.

We have to study demographics to save our democracy from populist forces that ferment anger and discontent. Unfortunately, the issue is still largely limited to academia, whereas I would like to see it discussed at our party conferences and in public forums. There are some very interesting studies that trace a direct correlation between the demographic crisis and the rise of populism. In fact, we should refer to populisms, in the plural, as they are composite in nature. There is economic populism, an intergenerational populism, and an ethnic populism.

ETHNIC POPULISM

The primary form of populism, perhaps the easiest to perceive, is ethnic populism. An ageing society, white and rich, finds itself having to interact with masses of non-white people (Arab, central African and Asian), who are often young and from cultures with higher birth rates. This is a problem familiar across Europe, from large cities that face riots in their suburbs, to the classic provincial city that sees more kebab shops opening than those selling pizza or crepes.

Ethnic populism is a phenomenon of great proportion, especially if we take into account that it comes in more than one variant. Not all European states have experienced the same type of migration over the same period, and certain ethnic groups have integrated more easily than others. Periodically, however, some ethnic groups, in particular, become part of the populist narrative. In Italy in the 1990s, for example, all the talk was of Albanians; then it was the turn of the north Africans. Today, alongside the concern prompted by the influx of refugees, at the centre of the news we find other groups such as the Roma.

The problem is always the same. Big demographic changes cause tensions in our societies. Sometimes these are hidden, and sometimes we don't even realise they are happening. For example, although we may see more elderly people, we might not realise the population is ageing. With issues regarding ethnicity, sometimes the issue is more evident. All it takes is for one Senegalese person to board a bus or train, and the perception immediately spreads that

European white people are on the verge of extinction. This is obviously not the case, but while studying it in school is simple, proving it in politics is a completely different matter. The central point is that ethnic change in Europe has only one path, and we cannot evade this fact: the white population is destined to grow old and dwindle; the non-white population is destined to grow considerably. To see this, all you have to do is watch a football match – and not just an Italian, French or German one. Let's take Switzerland as an example. In June 2015, for the important Euro qualifier against Lithuania, the 11-man Swiss team included players with names like Inler, Seferović, Xhaka, Behrami, Rodríguez, Drmić, Djourou and Shaqiri. Not exactly the grandchildren of William Tell. All Swiss, but of Albanian, Kosovan, Bosnian, and Ivory Coast origin. When it comes to dribbling around a centre-back and scoring a goal, we close our eyes to players' origins. Yet Switzerland is a country that in a 2009 popular referendum banned the construction of new minarets. The vote was pushed by rightwing political forces and the proposal was backed by 57 per cent of voters. In my opinion, this is one of the clearest examples of ethnic populism. The threat of cultural and religious diversity (in this case symbolised by minarets) is viewed as potentially dangerous and something to be fought. In a subsequent referendum, the Swiss also voted against allowing the free movement of European citizens, creating more problems for themselves than for those EU citizens – in particular those from Italy, France and Germany – by whom they evidently felt threatened.

Ethnic populism maintains that the prevailing ethnic group (in Europe's case, the white population) is under threat and it mobilises itself to preserve its identity. However, it is important to address this fundamental issue with care: one should never pit identity and integration against each other. In reality, the stronger people's identity, the better the conditions for real integration. Nonetheless, there remain those who claim that living with other ethnic groups is dangerous.

It is obvious that the question is not simply one of identity. There is also an economic aspect that causes antipathy and, in some cases, hatred. The resources given to migrants makes some automatically think that these benefits are being taken from 'us' (Italians, French, Germans, British – insert the nationality of your choice here) to be given to 'them'. Direct or indirect social expenditure on migrants is viewed by many citizens as a waste or, worse still, as theft. The notion that 'our' taxes are financing social housing, healthcare and other services for migrants becomes more widespread and the source of great animosity.

Populists add fuel to these flames, hoping to provoke a nationalist backlash and a reaction to the cultural diversity and the new European identity, which they fear and oppose. It is easy to blame Brussels for the problems associated with migration. The Italian populist Matteo Salvini, who is also a member of the European parliament, suggested that the hundreds of migrants landing in Reggio Calabria be loaded onto buses and transported to Brussels. Apart from the fact that boarding a bus to Brussels is something he himself might want to consider (he is rarely seen in the European parliament or in those parliamentary committees where the real work gets done), this is one of the many examples of how ethnic populism works. The populists find an enemy (the migrants) and someone on whom to pin responsibility (the EU), and they advocate that, by opposing both of them, things will improve (for the Italians, obviously).

Illusions mixed with demagoguery. But if a narrative like this gains traction it is because the alternative has not been properly examined. Our libraries are full of books on multiculturalism, typically produced in the 1990s, but are we sure that their arguments are valid, given the results they yielded? To create modern integration programmes, European policymakers need to go back to school, but possibly using new books.

ECONOMIC POPULISM

Populism takes on a more economic dimension when it seeks to appeal to those deemed the 'losers' of globalisation. In 1981, at the dawn of a new economic era, more than half the population living in developing countries earned less than $1.25 per day. By 2010, this fell to 21 per cent. In the course of a generation, approximately 25 years, the total number of people suffering from hunger fell from 18.6 per cent to 12.5 per cent of the world's population. Many proponents of the free market consider this data conclusive, and end the debate by stating that capitalism, liberalism and globalisation have brought billions out of poverty. The difficulty is that, when faced with improving the lives of billions of people, the pyramid remains tight and, while the poor are less poor, the rich are richer. A phrase uttered by the American billionaire Warren Buffet has stuck in my mind: "There's class warfare, all right, but it's my class, the rich class, that's making war, and we're winning." Buffet is anything but a conservative and his phrase is obviously meant as a provocation. I do not believe that the social classes are at war. I believe, rather, that it is the middle class with the greatest opportunities.

Yet, it is undeniable that in the last few years, which have been characterised by an acute crisis, the great majority of the population have begun feeling a double resentment. The first we addressed previously: a resentment towards migrants, whether driven by economics ('they are stealing our jobs!') or cultural issues ('we do not want their mosques!'). The second resentment is something relatively new in European society, which we have not experienced in a long time. The immense economic growth after the war, coupled with sustainable demographic growth, led many of us to get used to constantly rising living standards for all citizens. However, demography shifts and the recent economic crises threaten to leave us with an impoverished middle class, worried that it can no longer afford the quality of life to which it had grown accustomed. This is where a second resentment – one aimed towards the elite – stems from. In a society where wealth is becoming increasingly concentrated in the hands of a select few, where social mobility has ground to a halt, it is not surprising that anger is directed at those who have more. In Italy, this was inevitable. For too long privileges were passed off as rights, there was too much resistance to controlling spending, there was too must waste. The public saw all this while receiving public services that did not match up to the level of taxes we pay.

Populists have fed on these popular feelings. The leap from popular to populist is a short and not a particularly pleasant one. In Italy, the Five Star Movement has based its appeal on an economic populism that rests on pledges as unbelievable as they are harebrained. Never before have I felt that phrase by Abraham Lincoln was so apt: "demagoguery is the ability to dress unimportant ideas in important words".

If an ever-increasing part of the impoverished middle class find these arguments convincing, it is in part because other political forces were not previously able to tighten their belts, curb spending and, above all, react to the growing inequalities in society. At the heart of the right's conservative doctrine is the acceptance of inequalities. But what about the left? For too long we have accepted that globalisation was the antidote to any problem, but we were without solutions when we found that little had been done to mitigate the growing social inequalities and large disparities of wealth.

In response, the populist narrative has been unrivalled, reviving old slogans as well as creating some new ones. It has produced a long list of 'guilty' classes and institutions, in which it is difficult to distinguish between banks, multinationals, politicians, immigrants, special interest groups, and the EU. It has given free rein to the anger of a society unable to prosper as it did in the past and uncertain about the future. During the Brexit campaign, a phrase deployed by Michael Gove struck me: 'the people of this country have had enough of experts'. It suggested that the economists and other experts supporting the remain campaign were acting in bad faith. Not only was this not the case, but economic figures were clear, and they were right. However, this message resonated with people. In the US, Donald Trump won also because he presented himself as an anti-establishment, and he was able to attack Hillary Clinton by portraying her as a representative of Washington (and thus of the government bureaucracy) and of Wall Street (and thus the financial institutions). Much irony stems from the fact that Trump, after winning the election, appointed to his administration many bankers, politicians, lobbyists and chief executives of multinationals. This seems a long way from the idea of taking on the establishment. Whenever I think about these issues, I recall a meeting I had with the director of the European food safety authority who spoke, with great frustration, about a scientific study that had taken two and a half years but was swiftly undermined by a Facebook post disputing it.

INTERGENERATIONAL POPULISM

Populism is also capable of getting into the innermost cracks in our society, becoming intergenerational and pitting young against old, millennials against baby boomers.

The generation that emerged from the second world war found itself faced with an accumulation of rubble in Europe, but with a vision. That vision was the welfare state. In part as compensation for the atrocities endured during the conflict, in part as an insurance policy against totalitarianism, half the governments of Europe managed to win widespread support thanks to the welfare state. Its introduction was an extraordinary achievement through which we revitalised our societies. It was the guarantee that the state would help its citizens and provide them with opportunities, despite the tragedy of the recent past and the uncertainty of the postwar years. In exchange for these rights, Europeans rolled up their sleeves and began to rebuild what the bombs had destroyed. Not only did they rebuild it all, but they did so with thriftiness and sacrifice. Every social advancement was achieved through hard work; each small luxury was carefully considered. It was because of this that their children were able to consolidate their social status and in many cases improve it. No other generation in history has lived with the wealth and welfare rights that those who are now aged between 65 and 75 enjoyed. They had the opportunity to study and become professionals, seeing ever-increasing levels of social mobility.

Let's take a look at Italy. In the 1960s, the number of children women gave birth to started to fall: three was the average in 1946, falling to fewer than two by 1976. In these 30 years, Italy experienced its first demographic shock. It meant that, on average, quality of life continued to increase and social mobility worked well. These were the golden years of the welfare state – a system that allowed a child born into a working or middle-class family to rise and become part of the elite. But, slowly, this all began to end. Europe's population became increasingly older. Welfare resources increasingly shifted to cover pensions, with less available for education and research. A prime example of this is Italy or Greece, where the state pension system was one of the primary causes of Italy's sluggish economic growth and the near-collapse of the Greek economy. The pension schemes were more generous than one can imagine, with much less dedicated to the younger generation. The result is that the generation that had enjoyed the most benefits of the welfare state continued to maintain its standard of living, at the cost of our young people. A huge blank cheque was written, which someone at some point in time would have to pay. But in so doing, we ended up exchanging rights for privileges. Let's call a spade a spade. Retiring and drawing a pension is a right. Retiring at 52 years of age is a privilege.

The consequences of all of this are clear to Europe's citizens. They are growing old and fear losing that which they feel they have earnt but, at the same time, are incapable of giving to their children all that their parents left them. When faced with the high rates of youth unemployment we see in many parts of Europe, their children or, rather, now their grandchildren, are too angry to think about pensions. Their first concern is to find a job.

Here is where the populists start to make their insinuations. If ethnic populism is that which pits 'us' against 'them', intergenerational populism is that which slowly but inevitably tears our social fabric. It fans the flames, pitting the old against the young, telling the former that their rights and privileges are in danger because someone wants to remove them, while telling the latter that they will never have those same rights and privileges, so now they must fight to achieve them.

Curiously, these clashes are united by a common feature: anti-Europeanism. How many times have we been told that our rights are under threat because of some dictator in Brussels? Let's look at the recent negotiations to save Greece. In a climate that more closely resembled the derby atmosphere of a football match than a negotiation between institutions, pro-Greek forces within Europe publicly pointed out that the Greek governments were asked to make further cuts to their pensions. Memorable moments from that summer are the weekend drops of the 'Kalimera brigade', the group of Italian far-left politicians who flew to Athens to support Alexis Tsipras' Syriza government on the occasion of the referendum on whether to accept the economic bailout conditions. After taking selfies in Syntagma Square, they took a closer look and discovered that in 2015 many Greeks were able to retire at 56 years of age, and those in certain jobs could even retire at 52. As I said previously, is such a pension a right or a privilege?

Brussels simply dictating cannot work, but neither can those political forces that seek to take short cuts. The example of Syriza is telling. When faced with bankruptcy, Tsipras revised his position and agreed to look at some of the privileges that still existed in Greece. Some think he did this for Europe. I like to think that he did it for his country, and for the Greek young people who deserve the opportunity of a better future than the one the previous, irresponsible political class denied them. He acted with strong leadership and clear democratic legitimacy, with a referendum followed by a general election to approve his difficult decisions. He acted with courage – the same courage that too many European governments have been missing on too many occasions.

DEMOGRAPHY, SOCIAL JUSTICE, WELFARE – THE NEED FOR NEW IDEAS

Economic crisis. Political crisis. Demographic crisis. To get out of this rut, to find an antidote to populism, there is only one path – the European one. We will not overcome it as Italians, Finns, Danes or Slovaks. We will overcome it as Europeans.

Anti-Europeanism has long been one of the cornerstones of populism. Among all populist rhetoric – the economic, the ethnic, the intergenerational, and across the political spectrum from right to left – Europe is cast as the cause of all society's problems. This is false. One can, of course, say that the EU has not always been able to find the right medicine for our ills, or that it wasted too much time researching strange remedies, or that it raised our hopes without having the necessary courage to fulfil them.

I don't want to claim that all populists are equal – naturally, there are many differences among the various political movements. However, anti-Europeanism is preached by Ukip in Britain as much as Podemos in Spain, the French National Front and Polish nationalists as well as the fringes of the extreme left who quit established social democratic parties in Italy and Greece, fragmenting the left at the same time as they called for unity. We cannot forget either the neo-Nazis of Jobbik in Hungary and Golden Dawn in Greece or the ill-named Sweden Democrats. In Italy it is quicker to list the pro-Europeans than all those that oppose Brussels. The anti-EU brigade is a club with an ever-increasing membership, covering what we used to call the 'constitutional arch'. Like the old formations of Panini football figurines – from left to right, we find the extreme right Brothers of Italy, the Five Star Movement, exiles from the Democratic party, and what's left of the radical left. All are united in a desire to abandon their responsibilities, beginning with their call to leave the eurozone. All advocate an 'out' frame of mind: out of parties, of parliaments, of Europe – in other words, they are 'anti-policy', united in being out of touch with reality. Unfortunately for them, problems cannot be solved with a policy of being in or out of the euro. The magic tricks that Italian populists advocate – from the flat tax proposed by the Northern League to the Five Star Movement's citizenship tax – are unachievable with either the euro or with our old lira, unless one believes, as Pinocchio was convinced by the cat and the fox, that gold coins grow on trees.

Anti-Europeanism, coupled with an attachment to various kinds of conservatism, is the essence of all forms of populism in Europe: a desire to maintain the status quo in a society that is changing because of the demographic transformation I have discussed.

In his latest book, Giuliano da Empoli, a brilliant young European thinker, describes how populism works like an algorithm. It thrives on problems, which it amplifies, and, depending on the circumstances, offers simple solutions. On the same issue, those solutions could go to either the left or the right.

How can we escape this vicious circle? To start with, we must tell the truth, explaining time and time again that the reality is not that which populists describe. We need to argue that they are fighting for a society that no longer exists. And we must explain that, in doing so, they are only exacerbating existing social conflicts, conflating, without rhyme or reason, the problems faced by the elderly, the uncertainties of young people, the difficulties of integration, and the hardships of poverty. Their answers are simple, but they are not solutions. The economy is stagnating? Then let's return to the lira. The number of migrants is growing? Then let's close our borders. Time out please!

To recap. We are witnessing fundamental demographic changes. Europe's population is no longer growing and its only lifeline is that extended by migration, which can set a new course for youth and family policies. However, these changes are accompanied by enormous social and political problems, as we have witnessed to date.

We will emerge from this with a better Europe. Right, but how? Effective action against populism, a real antidote, starts with us taking stock of an enormous demographic transformation that involves more than 300 million people. It is an almost homogeneous condition throughout the 28 member states. Only France and Ireland have an above-average birth rate of two children per woman, and no country is below the level of 1.21. This shared problem has no national solution. Only a transnational approach will work, with shared decisions on welfare, integration and migration. We are still far from having common policies that can make a big difference, be they specific, like research and education, or more general, like fiscal policy. A common budget for the EU, for example, would be an important first step towards implementing public policies to sustain integration, or new social policies, like a European subsidy to fight unemployment, to complement national programmes. As a first step – following which many others must be taken – we need new money and new ideas.

What is the future for societies where the work of women is not adequately valued, where more and more young people are choosing not to have children? One response to the demographic change we are experiencing is the effective integration of migrants. But we cannot stop there. We also need to support the 30-year-olds, who we have asked to trust us, who we have asked to further their education firm in the belief that the investment will reap dividends. Unfortunately, this is not the case for everyone. It is unlikely to be the case, especially in Italy.

I recall a graph published by the Bank of Italy. Imagine in 1995 the average wealth of the head of each Italian household was pegged at 100. Today, those who are aged over 65 would have reached the level of 160. My generation is around the level of 90, while those aged between 18 and 34 are at the level of 40. This means millennials are at serious risk of not being able to buy a car. If they need a bank loan, they are likely to need their parents to act as a guarantor – and let's not even get into a discussion about their pension. Under such conditions, who would be mad enough to bring children into this world?

This situation is particularly acute in Italy but, unfortunately, we find similar problems – albeit with individual national nuances – across Europe. This is why we cannot only concentrate on integration. We also need adequate social and youth policies. Any working person – even someone earning the minimum wage or with little job security – should not view starting a family as an impossibility. This is particularly the case for women. In Italy, approximately a third of women give up their jobs following the birth of their first child. This is a statistic that should give us pause for thought as it indicates, unfortunately, our country trails far behind European norms.

By helping working women and families, ensuring they are supported by decent public services, governments can show they really care, not only about the future of their countries, but also about the current population. Naturally, social policy cannot be designed with a one-size-fits-all approach – each proposal must reflect individual societies and their relative needs. After much delay, the Italian government has started to provide new solutions in sectors where previous administrations responded with either cuts or a plethora of measures. The Employment Act, one of the most important reforms brought about by the Renzi government, ushered in a decisive change of course with regard to maternity policies. It stems from a belief in the principle of flexibility in maternity leave. This is an important change, allowing new mothers to choose either a career break or a shift to part-time work, and puts an end to 'forced resignations' – a very humiliating practice in our society.

The Employment Act also introduces a series of innovations in our welfare system. Our real challenge stems from the fact that the days are long gone when problems could be resolved with indiscriminate public spending. The difficulty we face, progressives in particular, is to guarantee the provision of good public services in a fiscally responsible way. This requires innovative ideas, like encouraging employer-provided welfare.

Best practice at an international – and, above all, European – level, suggests that effective social policies are those that involve local communities, in all of their complexities. Local government, but also co-operatives, non-profit organisations, and individual citizens. In many northern European countries, childcare providers, such as childminders, have become central figures in helping mothers to reconcile their work-life balance. This role is unfortunately absent in Italy, with the exception of the *Tagesmutter* (childminders) in Trentino-Alto Adige. Some suggest nursery schools are enough. Without doubt, nurseries remain the best solutions to these problems, but it is not easy to build them everywhere – especially in areas that are difficult to reach, such as rural or mountainous communities. Therefore, employing qualified maternal assistants may provide two benefits: providing many young people with jobs in this sector, while also helping families secure a better work-life balance.

There is an urgent need for solutions to the social crises we are witnessing in Europe, which are largely consequences of the economic crisis. Europe must help and support new families. We need to demonstrate our belief that the family unit is the foundation of our society. I should stress that I mean this to apply to every family – whatever the parents' sexual orientation. On this issue, despite our country being very late in adopting a modern stance relative to other European countries, Italy has now taken important steps forward, with the approval of a law on civil unions in 2016. Can we do more? Yes, but civil unions represent important progress, especially culturally, as we managed to overcome the ultra-conservative forces that are still present in Italian politics, but may be stuck in the wrong century.

A few years ago, I was struck by the words Britain's prime minister of the time, David Cameron, used to explain his support for the legalisation of same-sex marriage: "I don't support gay marriage in spite of being a Conservative. I support gay marriage because I am Conservative." I disagreed with Cameron on a lot of things, but this is a phrase that many of our old-fashioned politicians should learn by heart. If we really want to strengthen our society, make it more secure and less vulnerable to crisis, let us provide our citizens with certainty. Let us allow them to build families from which they can find stability and security.

Demographics, social justice, welfare – these are all challenges that must be faced with ideas. These ideas need to derive from the progressive movement, in response to the populists who are, at this historic moment, the real reactionaries in Europe. Modern pro-Europeans need to take a decisive leap forward. The social democratic model is in crisis and now, more than ever before, we need to find common solutions to problems that are increasingly complex. European reformers, especially those in government, have a duty to pay attention to the potential social conflicts that populists are trying to ignite, between generations, between social groups, between citizens and migrants. Across Europe, we see tensions that find their outlet in a drift towards populism. A movement like the anti-austerity *indignados* in Spain demonstrates the anger and frustration felt by a generation that is unsure of its future. As long as these protests find a voice in populist, but essentially democratic, movements like Podemos, the system holds up. However, when the answer is something like Jobbik or Golden Dawn, the system comes under strain.

This is why we must not give in to populism. Because the alternative would be collapse. Our society will become increasingly rancorous and violent, and less trusting towards outsiders – whether these be the elite institutions that rule above them or the newly arrived migrants who wish to join our society. This is not the kind of Europe we want.

LET US CONTINUE TO BE OURSELVES

We must take a deep breath before starting our discussion on Europe and the question of rights versus security, and the threats posed by terrorism. We must force ourselves to use our heads when there is a strong inclination to use our gut instincts. This is why we must pause for a moment: because the threat posed by Islamist terrorism is not only terrible in its own right, it also poses an existential threat to our society.

The subtle threat we face is that little by little, in the war on terror, we sacrifice our freedoms. Refusing to give into our fear is itself a challenge. If there is a terrorist attack on an underground train, our instincts sometimes tell us not to use that service any longer, even if using it is the most ordinary and mundane part of our lives. If attacks at airports continue, we may be tempted to no longer take exotic holidays because we think it is safer to remain at home. These are perfectly normal and understandable reactions, and we come to accept the increased security checks at airports, public places, and elsewhere. I have lost count of the number of times that I have been forced to pass through a metal detector over the last 15 years.

This is not the real risk. The risk is seeing our liberties slowly squeezed in a way that threatens our civilisation and our culture of rights that distinguishes us from other societies. This danger is the aim of the Islamist terrorists and all those who attempt to instil hatred into western society. They want to convince us that the only possible solution is to become a little less human, and a bit more like them. The terrorists want to kill us not so much for what we do, but for what we represent: for our values, our freedoms, and our liberties.

We must not give into fear. Living in fear is destructive: we forget all too quickly the value we place on our liberties and democracy, which are the foundations of our civilisation. If we do so, the terrorists will have beaten us at home, in the places we are supposed to be at our strongest and from which we should launch our fight back.

A sad example of the consequences of the nationalism that such fear perpetuates can be seen in the murder of Jo Cox. The violence that led to the death of the British pro-remain Labour MP during last year's referendum campaign must serve as a wake-up call. Nationalism, as Mitterrand told the European parliament in 1995, causes war between peoples and violence in our society. Jo's husband, Brendan, said after her death: "Jo believed in a better world and she fought for it every day of her life. She would have wanted all to unite to fight against the hatred that killed her. Hate doesn't have a creed, race or religion." We are with Brendan and with Jo. We are, and always will be, on the side of those who believe in freedom for all and of those who fight for it against violence. Killing a young woman who worked hard for her country was brutal. Killing her while screaming "Britain first" is even worse, as it means that nationalism is bringing death to Europe once again.

One of the last passages written by Pier Paolo Pasolini, the Italian film director and philosopher who was murdered 40 years ago, was the speech he planned to deliver to the Radical party conference in 1975. Instead, it was delivered in his absence to a shocked and saddened audience. Pasolini left us with one great lesson: "You don't have to do anything except to simply continue being yourselves." But what does being ourselves mean? It means that denouncing terror is not enough, being indignant about it is not enough. We must, first and foremost, respect ourselves more. We need to have more faith in our strengths and values, and we need to fight back. The first way to counter the violence that wishes to destroy us is to remain true to ourselves. When faced with these threats we must take back control of our lives.

BALANCING RIGHTS AND SECURITY

Unfortunately, we see more and more people in public life who do not need to be terrorists to behave inhumanely. Just switch on the TV, at any time of the day or night, to hear outrageous discussions by people who trade in hatred and demagoguery. As if closing down a mosque could stop the spread of extremist material online, or shutting down borders could be a solution when many terrorists are in fact homegrown.

Perpetuating the myth that all Muslims are Islamist fundamentalists or Muslim immigrants are outlaws is the best gift we can give to European Islamist extremists, pitting citizens against Muslims and thus pushing Muslims into the arms of fanatics.

We must urgently review our integration programmes in detail, as not all of them have been successful. Today, integration means giving young people in disadvantaged areas a reason to choose life over death and respect over violence. Much of the violence we see stems from a feeling of social exclusion, finding an outlet for this anger, and the perceived 'status' of martyrs in radical Islam. However, the violence is not only the result of social exclusion. It is also ideological in nature, as demonstrated by the many terrorists who come from well-integrated, middle-class families.

It is precisely because of radical ideology that this violence has been unleashed, against the Erasmus generation in particular. The vast majority of those 30- to 40-year-olds who were slain in the Bataclan were cosmopolitan, multilingual, had lived overseas and wanted to travel. It is our generation against whom those 20-year-old fanatics unleashed their hatred. This is a double challenge for us – because now we are now in positions of responsibility, and these radicals want to extinguish our way of being, our way of life. We must do all we can to stop them from doing so and to overcome this terrible challenge.

Valeria Solesin was an Italian, one of the 19 nationalities represented among those massacred on that horrible evening. Like Valeria, I once studied at the Sorbonne. I too knew the Bataclan and the 11th arrondissement – where I had once lived – well. I too love rock music: just like Valeria and Matthieu Giroud. Matthieu was a proud example of the Erasmus generation: a French academic who studied all over the world. That evening, he was at the Bataclan, a place from which he would never return home. Matthieu will never know the daughter his pregnant wife was carrying, and would never again see his three-year-old son Gary. This news filled me with pain and emotion. They want to deny us our liberties. We need to put an end to their violence. Dialogue will never be an option with them. We must fight with all our might to overcome them, but without forgetting our values.

Unfortunately, the balance between rights and security is becoming more difficult to strike. We face an enormous test: to safeguard our rights while remaining strong in the face of all forms of terrorist violence. I am convinced that a way to retain both the right to security and the security of rights exists. However, in order to achieve this, we must speedily and efficiently build a European security system. Schengen does not only mean freedom of movement. It also means border police, integration of our intelligence services, a real common security policy, a European CIA.

We have to accomplish all of this without renouncing our founding values. The reaction to the attacks in Paris in November 2015 demonstrated our solidarity and strong desire to remain united in the face of this terror. However, it was not long before the vultures and demagogues showed up. It's time for us to say that we are tired of those who try to sell false solutions like walls and barbed wire in the middle of Europe. We have to remind those who advocate expelling migrants that many terrorists have the same nationalities as us. If we start causing divisions among ourselves, we will be heading in the direction that the terrorists want us to. It is natural that, after a disaster of this kind, the desire to increase security is high, but we cannot sacrifice all we have on the altar of security. Security requires solidarity between us all as Europeans. Let us unite to overcome this global attack upon us. Yes, this is an enormous task, similar to the one our founding fathers faced in the 1950s, having lived through the second world war and the Holocaust. Let us remove the political scepticism, the bureaucratic resistance, the national self-interest.

That's right, self-interest. Immediately following the Bataclan attack, and the tragic attacks at Brussels airport, in Nice and the Christmas market in Berlin, there were those who took the opportunity to attack the European agreement on the relocation of asylum seekers – as though Syrian refugees were not trying to escape from exactly the same butchery at the hands of Isis. Unfortunately, the strategy of the Islamist extremists is precisely to divide us. Let us consider a few key facts: the Syrian passport found next to one of the suicide bombers in Paris, whether fake or not, led to fears that all refugees are potential terrorists. We have to respond firmly to this madness. Refugees and asylum seekers are running away from the same murderers we saw in action in the Bataclan (even if they had Belgian and French nationalities). This is why we have no option but to arm ourselves with resolve and courage, and counter every attack on our way of life.

Reaffirming our values and liberties should be our primary response. We should not renounce our way of life. Following the attacks on the London underground in 2005, Tony Blair uttered few, but very significant words: "They will never destroy our way of life." Never give into fear. Never change your way of life.

THE SECURITY WE WANT

Fear is like a worm that burrows deep into our psyche. Every parent struggles to sleep when their children are out dancing at a nightclub, with the fear that they will drink too much or get into a car accident.

Something new and profoundly dangerous is that we are afraid that we will have to get used to feeling this way. Israel has experienced countless terrorist attacks, but Israelis will tell you that nothing was ever the same again after the attacks on the Dolphinarium nightclub in June 2001, when 21 young people – mostly teenagers – were murdered in a suicide bombing. When the victims are adolescents who are just out dancing and having fun, it seems that there is no limit to this terror.

Immediately following the attacks on the Bataclan, the then president, François Hollande, declared a state of emergency (which Macron lifted two years later) and announced tighter border controls. It was a perfectly natural response, and we do not need to ask what our response to such an attack would have been instead, or what his alternatives were. The French reaction was strong and decisive. It was first and foremost a national response. However, in the face of this unprecedented attack, the clause on European solidarity found in the Lisbon treaty was also invoked for the first time. For the first time, therefore, the response was not 'only' a national one.

This aspect should be emphasised. Let us remember, we were attacked by a global monster, and by butchers who were both European and non-European. Thanks to our security services, we know that we face terror cells dispersed across various European capitals, which are organised, trained and directed by a leadership outside of Europe. The last attack on Paris was planned in Syria, put into action on Belgium, and executed in France. When faced with this type of unprecedented threat to our security, we need to respond with greater co-operation and solidarity as Europeans. Much has been done in Europe since the Charlie Hebdo massacre to increase co-operation in order to prevent attacks and other threats. But such progress, although very important, is still insufficient.

Security is a fundamental right that all those in government must guarantee to their citizens. However, security is too big a challenge to be dealt with solely at the national level. Only as Europeans can we contribute, together with the Americans and the Russians, as well as regional actors like Turkey and Saudi Arabia, to efforts to overcome this new unprecedented global threat, one which is made up of a transnational network of lone wolves.

European states must not succumb to passing national legislation in the mould of the Bush-era Patriot Act. If anything, the EU should pass a truly European act that includes all member states and takes our rights into consideration in the fight against terrorism. Because, I repeat, defending our security must also encompass the security of our rights. Many people fear that national constitutions are in danger of being amended to restrict our rights in the name of security. This is exactly what not to do. Certainly it is possible to amend laws, to update them and make them more compatible with the threats we face today. But this cannot be at the expense of a reduction in our rights. Law and order may be what we need, as long as law equals order. We all remember what happened in the United States after 9/11. In terms of human rights, Guantanamo and Abu Ghraib were some of the darkest prisons in recent history, and I believe that Guantanamo contributed nothing to reinforcing America's security and influence in the world.

So what should we do? We certainly need to raise our level of awareness and follow our guiding principle – security with rights. We must intensify co-operation between European police and intelligence forces. I see no valid reason why the Belgian police had intelligence that was ignored by the French in the case of the attacks in Paris. I am well aware that the civilian police and military intelligence services find it difficult to communicate, so we have much to do as we evolve from the co-operation to the integration of our intelligence services. If we still believe it is too hard to strengthen the exchange of intelligence between European secret services, think how long the road ahead of us will be to arrive at the one solution capable of delivering a lethal blow to transnational threats: a fully European intelligence service. More generally, countries in the civilised world should spend less time spying on each other and more time together fighting our all too real, common threats.

We must make a common security and defence policy our top priority and the cornerstone of European collaboration, because only together can we effectively respond to these new threats. We have to start by overcoming the usual objections raised on this subject. This is not about transferring our national armies and armaments to the EU. Nor does it mean that we will be asking our citizens 'to die in the name of Europe'. European identity does not come into it. We need to create integrated bodies of professional military personnel to respond to the new threats that we are facing, and to have the capacity to react with speed and effectiveness in the ever-increasing number of European crisis missions overseas – starting with those regions that are close to us and of strategic importance. Let's put our emotions aside and focus on our common interests. For some time now, nation-states have no longer been the sole military actors on the global stage. In this era of multilateralism, the EU needs to become a new military power, as well as a civilian one.

An integrated defence capability would increase our military power and reduce military spending in individual national budgets. A report in December 2016 by McKinsey calculated that if European nations pooled their procurement procedures when buying defence equipment, they would save 30 per cent of their current costs. If we combined the military expenditure of the 28 member states it would be greater than that of China, Russia, India, Japan, South Korea or Saudi Arabia. However, we have a military capability that is far less effective than that which the total combined expenditure would give us. Do we really wish to carry on having 28 separate armies, 24 air forces, and 21 navies? In the next 10 years, we need to develop a new European defence and security strategy, one that continues to work on stabilising the world and reacting to new threats such as terrorism.

Guaranteeing security also means being active online. Later on in this book, we will discuss how digitisation has improved and simplified our lives in ways that we are not even able to quantify. However, it is also evident that the threats we are facing today are increasingly proliferated online – due to not only the ease of digital communication, but also its speed. On WhatsApp alone, an unbelievable 30 billion messages are exchanged daily. It is clear, therefore, that this is our new battlefield. This is why we need to invest in cyber security – to map suspects and intensify controls. We must achieve all this, however, without causing any potential repression. In fact, digital security and technology is a perfect case study through which to examine the relationship between security and safeguarding rights.

Let us try to imagine the consequences if the response to a security problem, for example an online threat, was simply to reduce digital freedom. If a law was proposed to restrict citizens' freedom to use the internet, we could find ourselves embarking upon a legislative journey without any idea where we would end up. Reality is difficult to predict. We need to safeguard the rights of those who are surfing online and, at the same time, improve the tools we have to intercept terrorist communications, which are often on platforms such as Skype or PlayStation. Yes, Skype and PlayStation – the same tools used by our kids almost every day to communicate and play with their friends online, who are located all around the world. Can we really comprehend limiting this right? It's impossible. Therefore we need to invest in intelligence, cross-reference our data and use all the tools available to us to their maximum potential. If we upgrade our alert level, it is obvious that we also have to immediately exchange information and intelligence on the situation, not only for the sake of the Schengen system, but also for Europol, Frontex, and all the other relevant European entities.

Schengen is an excellent example of what we are discussing here. Everyone associates this treaty simply with the free movement of people without the need to carry a passport. This is absolutely correct, but we must not forget that Schengen is also a formidable instrument that could be used to fight the threats to European security together – yes, together! – from co-ordinating judicial bodies to co-operation between our police forces and effective control of our borders where it is really needed: on the external borders of the EU. In the last few years, many have criticised Schengen as the source of too much individual freedom. However, I think that we should criticise it for what it is not able to do, for the fact that we are not able to take advantage of its full potential to enhance our collective security and take full advantage of the opportunities it provides for.

Our borders are no longer two-dimensional outposts of the Westphalian state. With globalisation, our frontiers have become increasingly complex areas in which many actors – whose rights are increasingly less clear – act. Attempting to reinforce our national borders is not only futile, but also counterproductive in terms of attaining our security goals. Let's make no mistake: the borders we have to work on, with greater speed and determination, are not those between member states. Our task is to concentrate on the European border, and to do so we need a truly common European border policy.

THE RIGHTS WE WILL NOT RENOUNCE

The threat we face is that of Islamist terrorism, which wants to splinter and destroy our communities – communities in which there are also people who share the Islamic faith. Immediately following the carnage in Paris, Muslims in many European cities held demonstrations. This was a very important move, because the most forceful and decisive rejection of the terrorists has to come from Muslims. Terrorists, in many cases, are attacking the communities in which they grew up, as second or third generation migrants. We appeal to these communities to act courageously and condemn with their words and actions the barbarians who seek to use their religion as an outlet for their hatred and madness. Muslims in Italy and throughout Europe must condemn these barbarians with no equivocation. Our enemies are found, first and foremost, within our own societies, within our own borders. They wanted to destroy freedom of expression. Some tried to excuse the attacks against Charlie Hebdo by stating its cartoons were a 'provocation'. That argument is unacceptable. Our right to security must never put our freedoms at risk; all our freedoms must be protected, including the right to publish satire that some may find offensive.

We expect a lot more from European Muslims. In the first demonstrations organised after the Bataclan attacks, some had the courage to take to the streets and shout before the media Isis is a cancer. This was a very important first step, but more is still needed. Everyone – but above all European Muslims – need to forcefully and without equivocation denounce the Islamist extremists, and show respect for our democracy, for secularism and for the open and tolerant societies that we wish to remain. Our society is based on fundamental rights that exist to benefit everyone who chooses to be part of it. On this, we must all insist.

Europe, our Europe, cannot give in to this blackmail. The election of Labour's Sadiq Khan, a second-generation immigrant and Muslim, as mayor of London in May 2016 made headlines. We should try to ensure that such a story is no longer newsworthy. When we reach a place where a person's faith is no longer news and we are able to stop using phrases like 'British Muslim' or 'French Jew', we will all be a bit more European and a bit more free. Until such a time, we need to make one thing clear: the constitutional freedoms, both the right to believe and to not believe, are equal in dignity, with a clear separation of state and religion. To any who do not understand this, we must explain that this is a non-negotiable right, and it is they who have to adapt to the values and freedoms enshrined in our constitution, and not vice versa. It is therefore clear that our integration policies have to achieve more and do better.

Speaking of rights in Europe in 2017 is by no means an easy task. The discussion has to begin with a discussion of what type of world we want. I believe this is a world in which we seek to achieve greater freedoms, and in which we safeguard and continuously update them. Numerous conflicts have left our societies increasingly torn over which civil rights and freedoms are valuable and therefore must be safeguarded.

Our Europe is under immense pressure. On the one hand, calls for more rights and freedoms are constantly on the rise. In Catholic Ireland, the incredible referendum held in 2015 saw a huge majority of citizens vote to legalise same-sex marriage. On the other hand, we see an ever-increasing number of countries where rights are under threat. The clearest example is Hungary under Viktor Orbán. This is a clear sign of the difficult times through which we are living and the increasing support for the far right, which we also see in Poland. Ultra-nationalists in government, neo-Nazis in parliament. Karl Marx was right when he said that history repeats itself, first as tragedy, then as farce. Unfortunately, that farce is being played out now, and sounds extremely dangerous. All one has to do is to read the political programmes of these parties to understand the challenge they pose to our democracy. It is a dangerous farce. I have experienced it – thankfully only in the form of verbal aggression – from a Jobbik parliamentarian during a meeting of one of the committees of the European parliament in 2013. It is difficult for me to forget the insults and the verbal abuse directed at me by a Hungarian member of the European parliament when we began discussing the human rights situation in Hungary and the dangers posed by rising antisemitism in the country. Likewise, I will not easily forget the looks on the faces of the rabbis and Jewish citizens who I met in Budapest in 2011, together with a group of European and Israeli parliamentarians, among them Fiamma Nirenstein, then an Italian parliamentarian. Antisemitism has returned to our continent. Our generation has no option but to fight it with all the force needed to defeat it.

The challenge we are facing is even more extensive than that: at what point do liberal democracies stop tolerating a lack of recognition of basic rights both at home and in neighbouring countries? Immanuel Kant wrote that "a violation of rights in one part of the world is felt everywhere". For how long are we going to accept Europe's return to the practice of erecting walls and other barriers to protect an undefined 'us' from an undefined 'them' – a 'them' that is in fact desperate people fleeing from war and other atrocities? How much are we willing to give up? How many of our rights are we willing to give up in the name of our right to security? My answer is none. I am convinced that securing our rights and the right to security must always progress together, in parallel.

I have lived in many parts of Europe, and especially in Paris. When I used to live there, and every time I go back, I always stop at one of the few big bookshops left in Saint-Germain: L'Ecume des Pages. Some years ago that bookshop had a shop window devoted Stefan Zweig. Zweig, deprived of his Austrian nationality by the Nazis because he was Jewish, fled to Brazil. From there, he described the double collapse of Europe: first in the Great War and then with the rise of Nazism. How does he describe the collapse of European values, which after his death in 1942 manifested itself in the final horrors of the Holocaust? He analyses the unconsciousness of his hometown, Vienna. In his memoir, "The World of Yesterday: Memories of a European", he writes, "Now that the great storm has long since smashed it, we finally know that that world of security was naught but a castle of dreams; my parents lived in it as if it had been a house of stone". I would never want to wake up one day and realise that our values stand on dreams and not on stone.

Europe has always been a continent that has fought for rights and freedoms. From the Magna Carta to the Bill of Rights, from the Declaration of the Rights of Man and of the Citizen to the European Convention on Human Rights. We have a multi-secular tradition that we must maintain and pass on to future generations. Above all it must be passed on to the generation that is building today's Europe. A generation that hasn't yet found all the answers it is looking for (for example, on the issues encountered in the debate on citizenship in Italy and other European countries) and is seeking to join the political debate.

If I had to think of one particular moment in the last few years when I was absolutely convinced that the future of our rights was guaranteed, it would be during the year 2000, when the Nice declaration came into force. It was a fundamental text from not only a legal point of view but, above all, it represented a political manifesto and action plan of great importance. Shortly afterwards, we experienced 9/11 and then attacks in the heart of Europe from Madrid to London, without forgetting Copenhagen. This forced us to reflect again on how to find the right balance between our rights and our security.

Today, 18 years after the Nice declaration, we ask ourselves why the fight to attain and affirm our rights was so important. Politics must accompany society on the road to attaining new rights and freedoms, because we must remember that the true recognition of rights and freedoms occurs *in itinere,* as is so splendidly affirmed by Article 3 of the Italian constitution. Not only do all citizens have equal rights, but it is also the duty of the republic to remove any obstacles to their freedom. Claiming their rights is a process, not simply a statement.

We do not want to give up any of our rights. We should not have to give up any of our rights. We must not give up any of our rights. This has even greater significance if we consider that in western countries (although not only in the west) we have witnessed an ongoing demand to strengthen our democracies. We all remember the huge controversies stirred by the NSA and the many protests that accompanied the approval of Ceta (the EU-Canada free trade agreement). Meanwhile the Transatlantic Trade Investment Partnership is never likely to be approved.

Speaking of Canada: easyJet does not operate on transatlantic routes, but if it decides to rethink that, Justin Trudeau will certainly be part of the reason. The Canadian prime minister is a global example to liberals: he has no fear in strongly defending his positions, whether they concern migrants, civil rights or free trade.

Without discussing individual cases, it is evident that an ever-increasing number of Europeans are paying attention to issues relating to their privacy, individual rights, and the transparency of economic and political decision-making in their own countries. It has not escaped our attention that it is the youngest members of society, the millennials, who are most sensitive to these issues. The truth is that a new European generation is being formed, one that does not wish to compromise on these matters. They are right.

It is certainly true that many countries now provide their citizens with more and more tools to access information, for example through the Freedom of Information Act. Nevertheless, it is also true that this is not the case everywhere and that very often these law do not live up to the natural and legitimate expectations of citizens. The right to know what those in government are doing in our name might improve the relationship between institutions and their citizens. Only a constant strengthening – not weakening – of the instruments and mechanisms available to citizens to hold governments to account will result in more robust and healthy democracies, thus reinforcing respect towards human rights.

A right to knowledge, based on obligations to notify, publish and put information in the public domain leads to a more informed citizenry and fairer decisions. We need to build a new human rights policy. This call to action is even more urgent when one considers the enormous amounts of data, information and knowledge-based tools that advances in technology have made available to us. Transparency is a necessary precondition for any democratic regime. This is as true for states as it is for supranational organisations, from the EU to the UN. We must certainly take into account our security needs but, to achieve improvements, we need to share more from European databases and provide all our police and national intelligence services with access. There should be a guarantee that the information contained within them is destroyed after a predetermined period of time and when the specific danger has passed. Moreover, its use must be strictly limited to preventative and investigative operations.

A better democracy is one in which there is an unceasing fight for the recognition and affirmation of rights, even when this causes clashes and conflicts between people of diverging views. I am not afraid of the clashes that may arise in the fight to attain new rights. Let us remember the heated debate, especially in Italy, that accompanied the fight for civil rights in the 1970s (such as the legalisation of divorce and abortion) or, indeed, how complicated and difficult it was to get certain principles adopted at a European level – for example regarding workers' rights. These debates do not worry me. What worries me is the exact opposite: it is indifference.

We need to be careful that these important battles are not put on the back burner because we assume that the public is not interested enough to fight for, or even to enter into a debate about, the need to reaffirm the rule of law. Just think of all the work that still needs to be done on gender equality, religious tolerance, and ensuring the right to a fair judicial proceeding. This is why we need a politically active engaged society.

Even in Europe – actually, above all in Europe – we must return to the question of the rule of law. During the Italian presidency of the EU in the second half of 2014, the Italian government led the fight to establish a mechanism to monitor the rule of law in member states. It managed to achieve a commitment by the EU council of ministers to go further in the debate and introduce checks on the rule of law within our union. This was one of the more important achievements of our presidency. It is an ongoing process and, in May 2017, we moved from words to deeds. During the general affairs council, the European commission examined the status of human rights in Poland. It was a constructive debate, which saw the commission asking to be updated on the recent reforms approved in Warsaw. It was thanks to the Italian presidency that the council was reminded of its responsibilities towards ensuring the rule of law. Indeed, the rule of law is one of the pillars of the EU, included in the treaties, and reaffirmed in the declaration of Rome of 2017.

The reason behind our commitment is very clear. It is the continuing need to oversee and safeguard our rights, be they the right to security and the rights of young people, or more traditional rights: freedom of expression, respect for minorities, gender equality, and the fight to end discrimination against vulnerable groups. These are the challenges that the EU must address. I am convinced that if every citizen were engaged in a free discussion on these issues, we would win the battle against fear and secure the continued strengthening of our fundamental rights in every aspect of public life.

BORDERS

The effort to balance rights and security is potentially required in every area that we see rights being abused or where we believe that our security is under threat. In particular, our policies need to focus on the peripheries of our world – our borders – because that is where the key challenges of our time are most striking. Let us return to some fundamental questions: who manages rights and security at our borders? Who has privileges and who does not? Which actors should be responsible for monitoring this?

Today an Australian student can purchase a book on Amazon and, within a few days, it will be delivered from England. A young person from Milan can travel throughout the EU by Interrail without needing a passport (something those who advocate the abolition of Schengen should consider). Similarly, there are scores of other examples that demonstrate that the concept of borders has slowly been weakened.

For centuries the borders of a state symbolised its power. Within that border, the state exercised a monopoly on power; it enforced taxation and maintained an army. Beyond that border there extended an area where the state had no power, so much so that borders were mythologised and made immortal in epic literature – from the Pillars of Hercules to Julius Caesar's Rubicon. History, our history, is marked by lines that cannot be crossed and whose limits had to be respected.

Naturally, this is not only true of physical limits. The entire process of creating a national identity, the feeling of belonging to a community, came about through a process of exclusion. We are not this, and therefore we must be that. We do not speak this language, we do not mint this currency, we do not believe in that god. Those who were not part of the group legitimised those who were in it. Nations were created through exclusion and were subsequently reinforced on the basis of this exclusion.

European history has been constantly forged by frontiers. There was a time when, after the 'new world' was discovered, European countries referred to the pope the question of where and how to draw a new border. Alexander VI and Julius II established that anything east of Cape Verde were lands that belonged to Portugal and anything that lay to the west belonged to Spain. That line became known as the *rava* (Portuguese for border) and is perhaps the strongest symbol of the politicisation of borders. Even before the erection of walls, a political decision divided the known world and created a border where none previously existed.

Modern European history has seen, on the other hand, a constant increase in the number of borders. Just think of the Congress of Vienna. Diplomats from all over the continent met to put back on a map all that Napoleon had swept away. The consequence of this was the return of nationalism, discontent with the new borders, and an imperialist path that led to two great wars.

It was only in the years following the second world war that things started to change. Paradoxically, on the one hand Europe was split in two by the scar known as the iron curtain. But, on the other hand, were those who worked incessantly to demolish this border. It is from this time that the project for European integration was launched. The cold war continued, and the Berlin Wall was erected, but, thanks to a handful of enlightened people, we were able to look beyond this and begin the process of integration.

The wars Europe has experienced in its history are unequalled anywhere else on earth. For centuries, Europe experienced violent bloodshed and death on its borders. Europe in its entirety has almost never experienced peace, with whole regions being theatres of war from the Roman age until the second world war. Notwithstanding this, war and peace, conflict and trade formed a certain dynamic within Europe. The history of the continent developed within this land, thanks to the free circulation of goods and ideas. This is what allowed Europe's nation-states to impose their values and virtues on the rest of the world: internal dynamism and an impressive desire to move around and expand by crossing and redefining borders.

However, there was a time in European history when all of this was placed in doubt. The Berlin Wall was not just an expression of the dictatorship that divided Germany in order to preserve its totalitarian regime. Its erection was also alien to our continent's history. The Berlin Wall represented a desire to freeze a border, to freeze a nation, to freeze a continent. The wall was the peak (or abyss) of this attitude. This is why, with the end of the cold war, we were convinced that our future was one without borders, barriers, doors, confines. It is no coincidence that so much time and effort was spent on demolishing the barriers inside our society, from inequality to discrimination. We really worked to translate into political action that beautiful speech on 'new frontiers' delivered by John F Kennedy over half a century ago.

FROM GAMES WITHOUT BORDERS TO LONG DISTANCE CALLS

There is much evidence to support the idea that we are heading towards a world without borders. First, this is seen in the advancement and speed of new technology. It took decades for us to do away with expressions such as 'long distance calls' and now the rapid spread of new communication technologies has suddenly accelerated a phenomenon that makes borders less politically significant. All of a sudden, we care less about customs controls, what documents we hold, how much money we need to convert into another currency. We travel without thinking about which airline would take us around Europe, the nationality of our university professor, or where the sweater we bought on eBay was made.

Thinking about this, it is not so much the borders that have disappeared but the control exercised over them. Our politicians find themselves with fewer and fewer tools at their disposal. Just think about the two pillars upon which European nation-states' sovereignty was founded – currency and the army. We have done away with the former and the latter is no longer as relevant as it was decades ago.

It is the institution of war itself that demonstrates how far the concept of national frontiers has been weakened. Around the world, conflicts take place less at 'the front' and more within the state. If, in past centuries, wars changed borders, today everything takes place within pre-defined borders. We see this in the ethnic wars of the

1990s, in the former Yugoslavia as well as in Africa, and with the latest examples in Libya and Syria.

In short, we have witnessed a weakening of state control over our borders for a number of reasons. Many global actors – including the huge scale of people, goods and capital that cross the borders between states and continents on a daily basis – are weakening the concept of borders. All this was accompanied by the decreasing ability of government to deal with fundamental issues relating to borders. We see this in the privatisation of transport services and the use of private contractors to manage borders.

Naturally, our policies have adapted themselves to these global social changes. Let us take the Schengen treaty as an example. It represents a huge victory and a milestone in European history. It is a case where politicians and governments understood their role, took stock of social changes around them and decided to respond accordingly. Through the principle of free movement, they diluted borders and augmented the European space.

Were we able to effectively manage these changes? We certainly tried. The EU's cohesion policy, for example, represents a response that has sought to transcend borders by working with areas and regions without consideration of traditional state boundaries. This, moreover, is a policy that, over the past 30 years, has mobilised billions of euros and created a link between Brussels and the individual regions. Despite its limitations and some inevitable mistakes that were made along the way – it is always right to question if a cohesion policy is still required – it was an innovative approach that contributed to the 'Europeanisation' of the EU's economic and social development.

The EU suddenly found itself with millions of its citizens crossing borders within it on a daily basis to work or study in other member states. This surmounting of internal borders acted as an accelerator to two other phenomena: the development of policies aimed at Europe's own citizens and the fact that Europe acted as a 'draw' for people travelling from other states.

Let us think of Europe's many citizens who live, work and study in other European states and of the degree to which we have had to adapt our laws and social policies in order to react to their needs – needs that did not even exist 10 years ago. Europe has had to find solutions in the areas of labour laws, pensions, insurance. European society, which evolved within a relatively well-organised programme, founded on relatively secure guarantees, has had to legislate and make judgements on issues as it enters unknown territory. Yet again we are dealing with pan-European policies, with judicial decisions that must be taken at the European, not national, level.

At the same time, the freedoms achieved within the EU created a fatal attraction. The world without borders that we built acted as an irresistible magnet for those who lived outside and wished to become part of it. Towards the end of the 1990s, we arrived at a point where economic and monetary union was complete and Schengen had been established; it really seemed as though a new world had opened up to us, under appealing slogans such as the 'new economy', 'globalisation' and so on. In 1999, we saw the end of a very popular television show called 'Games Without Borders'. To many it seemed outdated with its teams of Italians playing Spaniards, Hungarians against Germans and so on. In a Europe without borders, there was no need for such games.

A WORLD IN SMITHEREENS

Suddenly, the world that we thought we had created shattered into smithereens. 11 September 2001 represented the end of the society to which we had grown accustomed. It brought on nightmares, fear and worries. And, as has always happened at the most important points in history, this had an impact on security, tolerance and innovation. Conservatives are defined by their desire to retreat and return to the old ways among which, obviously, are our old borders.

Naturally, the events of 9/11 were not the sole cause of all of this. But if we think back to 1998 when, following the Good Friday agreement, many of the barriers that still dominated Northern Ireland were dismantled, it is clear the beginning of the 21st century marks the start of a different era. All over the world, we find examples of new walls being erected.

Take Tijuana, on the border between the United States and Mexico, where the Bush administration ordered the border be reinforced as a wall in 2006, to combat illegal migration, drug trafficking and violence. It is one of the longest walls in the world, at a length of more than 3,000 km and costing $2.5bn in total to build. According to the Mexican commission on human rights, by 2011 more than 5,600 people had died trying to cross it.

Look at the West Bank in 2001. Blocks of cement, more than four metres high, separate this region from the state of Israel – a wall that was declared illegal in 2004 by the International Court of Human Rights in The Hague.

India and Pakistan, 2003. Two large emerging states, each in possession of the atomic bomb, put down a barbed wire fence that spans almost 3,000 km along their border.

And then we then come to Europe. The continent of the Berlin Wall is turning back the pages of its own history. We should not forget the wall in Nicosia, erected 30 years ago in Cyprus and symptomatic of an open wound. It is incredible how quickly many countries in the last few years have returned to the practice of marking their borders. In November 2013, Bulgaria approved the construction of a fence along the border with Turkey to counter the surge in immigration from the Middle East. We obviously cannot remain silent about the wall of barbed wire ordered by Viktor Orbán along the border with Serbia. Four meters high and designed to stem the tide of those who are trying to flee from war and tragedy. I find incomprehensible what we in Italy call Austria's 'waltzing'[1] – its indecision and threats to build barriers on the Brennero border. Given that Italy and Austria have shown they can co-operate on a range of issues in the past, I cannot think of a reason for this, other than electoral calculations.

The question of borders is such a big issue that it does not only concern immigration. However, immigration, which we have already discussed, is the primary phenomenon associated with borders today. All the aforementioned walls – and one should remember that since 1991, or the end of the cold war, 27,000 km of new walls have been erected in the world – were created with the aim of combating illegal migration and reinforcing national security. There is no doubt that Israel considered these factors when deciding to construct the wall with the West Bank, and that India wanted to protect itself from Pakistan following the terrorist attacks of 2001.

In certain circumstances, the idea of constructing a barrier to isolate oneself is an appealing option, particularly when dealing with an undemocratic government. But democracies also have a strange attraction towards walls: the United States, Israel, Bulgaria, Hungary and India are all democracies that have erected borders with great ease. Left and right do not come into play here. The decision to build a wall has nothing to do with a particular political force. The desire to return to borders is found throughout the modern world, especially in parts of the world marked by a decade of tension, fear and conflict, be it economic or political.

National governments have reclaimed their borders, and they have done so politically. Erecting walls, be they made of bricks or barbed wire, is a purely political act. This is especially the case when it is done following years during which those borders have generally become less significant on the international stage. In Europe, the continent of the iron curtain, this brings with it an additional problem. The return of a border policy is accompanied by a strong effort to reassert national policies to exert control over these same borders. There wouldn't be anything wrong with this. Indeed, it would be entirely legitimate were the EU to decide to launch a common border policy (I will return to this point later). However, the problem is that Europe is unable to react with the required consistency and speed and, more often than not, it is the member states themselves who put into practice schizophrenic and contradictory policies. I do not think it makes sense that within the same union we find one state that says it will open its borders to all the asylum seekers that cross it, while a neighbouring state starts building barbed wire fences to prevent those same migrants from setting foot on their soil. This is the consequence of the lack of a common policy on the subject of borders. The lack of transnational action forces all decisions to be taken at the national level. We are well aware of the risks: a tragic domino effect, the result of which will be the closing of all borders.

EUROPEAN BORDERS

How do we get out of this situation? We dreamed of a Europe without borders, but we find ourselves in a continent in which barriers and walls are on the rise. As always, we must begin with a reality check. We can see that over the last few years crossing Europe's borders has become more difficult and complicated, even for citizens travelling by train, let alone for asylum seekers or migrants.

We must then resolve the crisis of trust that is affecting the EU. This is the fundamental issue: if there is a lack of trust between one nationality and another, or between one state and another, how do we avoid imprisoning ourselves within our own borders?

This is more than an abstract question. I have participated, together with Renzi and Gentiloni, in almost all of the European council meetings held over the last three years, and I clearly noticed the effects of a lack of trust between our governments. Whether we were discussing Greece, migration or budgetary policies, the atmosphere was one of a club in which some members feel the others are trying to trick them. This makes everything, even that which common sense dictates should be easy, much more complicated than it has to be, such as coming together to protect our borders jointly.

There is a particularly odious and iniquitous facet to the way nationalists have politicised our borders – the fact that limitations are only being imposed on human beings. If I wish to make a bank transfer between Serbia and Hungary, I can do so with a click of my tablet. The same goes if I wish to buy a product – a container full of goods, including my package, will arrive at destination within a couple of days. But when we are dealing with human beings, this ease vanishes, and freedom of movement is curtailed harshly.

Prominent students of biopolitics, notably Michel Foucault, have examined the power politicians exercise over people, especially their bodies. That's right, their bodies. At least 20 years have passed since Europe was shaken by the sight of corpses buried in mass graves in Srebrenica. But today we all see corpses once again, the victims of unacceptable tragedies. There are also those 'lives laid bare', those who are alive but forgotten: the human beings that try to escape hostile governments or conflict in their home countries but find themselves stuck in national frontier lands or refugee camps.

What emerges, yet again, is a question over what our concept of a border is. What was originally a relatively simple point of separation has, over recent decades, become a grey area, a 'bubble' in which it is unclear where the state's power starts and the citizen's freedoms ends. Within this bubble power is not only exercised by the state, but by a multitude of actors – from people traffickers to smugglers and armed militias to terrorists – who exercise de facto power and force.

How long will we continue to accept this? It should be clear that we are at a crossroads. One road leads us to an ever-increasing assertion of national control over our borders. We know all too well where this road will lead us: in the short term to the end of Schengen and the disintegration of Europe. We will return to a Europe of nation-states, separate from one another, then against one against the other. We know where this story ends.

But there is also another road – one where we do not consider our borders as political confines, but rather as lying at the heart of our policies. To this I wish to add one adjective – European. This is the key. Let us discuss borders, but let us do so together. Let us introduce constraints and, if necessary, increase security measures. But we must not ignore the chaos Europe has found itself over the last few years.

Are left and right the same when dealing with the issue of borders? If we think of the EU today, we can see that this is an issue that crosses political boundaries. Governments led by conservatives (such as Germany's) have taken courageous decisions on this subject, which were somewhat unexpected. At the same time, countries with left-leaning governments, such as Slovakia and the Czech Republic, chose to close their borders, acting in a self-interested way.

I feel that we have not discussed this subject enough, just as we do not discuss the question of demographics enough, as we saw in the previous chapter. We cannot start talking about borders only at the point where we have thousands of refugees and immigrants amassed in Ventimiglia, just as we cannot start discussing the issue of demographics only when we realise that, without the contribution of immigrants, European societies will not be able to stand on their own two feet.

Let's talk about the issue of borders, but let's do so seriously. There was a time when we used to talk of the 'border line'; today we have to recognise that the word 'line' no longer sufficiently captures a reality that is much more complex. In time and space, borders have been diluted. We thought we had overcome them, but they returned. If we do not start discussing them again, if we do not quickly orient political action towards the question of borders, we will arrive a minute too late, just after the last section of barbed wire is laid.

NOTE

1. *Giro di valzer*, literally 'waltzing' in Italian, means to change one's mind very quickly. Similar to the expression 'flip-flopping' in English.

THE DIGITAL OPPORTUNITY

If it is true that, each day, Europe has to tackle important crises that are critical to its survival, it is also the case that, if it cannot see beyond the day-to-day, it will become simply an administrator, managing these issues. It will slowly diminish in importance as it becomes increasingly irrelevant politically and is faced with increased indifference on the part of its citizens. This would be a massive defeat, especially in light of our incredible history. We will miss out on huge victory if we do not recognise the incredible opportunities that technological advances provide us with today.

Looking towards our future means doing everything possible to ensure that the EU embarks upon a path of innovation. The digital change we are seeing is without a doubt a revolution that is capable of changing our society even more than the industrial revolution we studied in our history books. Naturally, innovation is not all that is required. Imagination and courage are also needed. This reminds me of a project launched in Zambia by Cisco, which is one of the nicest stories associated with what is known as the 'internet of things'. Thanks to a special GPS, the creators of this project were able to trace the movements of elephants, to control their displacement and thus ensure that they did not end up in the hands of poachers. I now ask myself a very simple question: have we realised the infinite potential we have before us? If we are able to defend elephants in Zambia, what other immense opportunities could we have to improve our own lives, and how many more such opportunities will arise for our children, the real digital natives?

THE FIBRE OF THE LEFT

Whether we like it or not (and, personally, I like it a lot) the transition towards a more digital society has already commenced. Some will certainly try to slow down this journey but, in the words of the Chemical Brothers, 'my finger is on the button ... push the button!' We cannot stop and forget about the potential of the innovation button. As Europeans we have a great opportunity to take advantage of the digital age in order to create a more inclusive society, which improves the lives of our citizens and produces new jobs in areas that until recently not only did not exist, but which we could not even have imagined.

Until 20 years ago, if I wanted to plan a holiday, I would have to drive to the travel agent; return home with a number of brochures and, having looked through them, call hotels and tourist offices. Then I would need to return to the agency, book the holiday and ask for further information about additional tours and excursions. Today, I can do all of this – and a number of other daily tasks – from the comfort of my own home with just a smartphone or tablet in hand. To paraphrase Humphrey Bogart's character in 'Deadline' – 'it's the digital age, baby!'

At this point, we must ask, will the digital revolution actually improve our lives?

Before answering, we need to take a step back. Over the last three years, I have worked directly on the establishment of the digital single market and have had the opportunity to participate in many meetings and workshops about innovation. I have noticed is that, up until last year, everyone was excited about the new opportunities of the technological revolution. However, since 2016 and the election of Donald Trump, we have concentrated on the negative side-effects of the revolution. Radical solutions have even been put forward, like taxing robots, which are seen as causing job losses.

This is a critical issue. As in the past, we should not adopt conservative positions now. Let's think about it this way. We are all very happy when with a simple 'click' we are able to order Japanese food to our home and it arrives at our door 20 minutes later. The job of politics, however, is to consider the rights and the salary of the delivery person. This is what social movements in our society should be concerned about.

The approach of a reformist left, in this case, needs to be balanced. We cannot stop the process of technological progress, but we cannot risk it pushing our society backwards. I understand this is not easy. To extend the previous example of a food delivery company, the first step is to establish what a collaborative economy is and to answer the question of how we define a platform, and so on. However, we also need the EU to be firmer, and progressive political forces have to speak up. We cannot be among those who protect special interests, but we also cannot be among those content to let the negative effects simply wash away the opportunities of an entire generation.

The technological revolution is radically changing our lives and the organisation of our society. History teaches that one cannot stop a revolution in its tracks, but that does not mean we should ignore those who remain excluded by that same revolution.

To paraphrase the Czech poet, Rainer Maria Rilke, we can say that digital innovation transformed us long before we were aware of it. Expressions like 'startup', 'sharing economy', 'digital platform', 'net neutrality' and many others entered our daily discourse without needing laws allowing this or banning that. Simply put, an increasing number of people in this digital society have decided that the advantages that derive from BlaBlaCar or Spotify are much greater than the things they are giving up. Talk of blocking digital development through protectionist measures is wrong, and also delusional. We need to create a digital society that is free and fair.

Of course, the spread of technology does not only benefit individuals. As we will see, digital innovation is one of the most important tools we have to develop a stronger economy, with higher growth rates and lower unemployment levels than Europe faces today.

It should be, in my opinion, a central theme of our public debate. The reason for this is simple: investing in the development of digital technology and, above all, in its spread, means investing in improving the daily lives of our citizens. Bringing broadband to every corner of Italy – and Europe – requires investment in fibre-optic rather than copper, to increase internet connection speeds to over 30mps. If we put the technical discussions aside, we can immediately see the obvious advantages of these decisions. A business using fibre-optic can get online much faster, thus increasing its potential markets and its ability to interact more quickly with government. Not only does all this serve as an incentive to businesses that are already operating in Europe, it also represents a big stimulus for startup and young people who dream of bringing new businesses to the market. At the same time, faster communication with government allows quicker responses to requests, or even simply accessing information. Enormous advantages could also exist for schools, clinics, training centres, and other public services.

Bringing broadband to our suburbs and rural areas, reducing bureaucracy, and educating young people to use these technologies are means to bring about social justice and provide equal opportunity for all. Offering equal opportunity to as many people as possible – this is the fundamental message of the net. It is also the fundamental message of a left that knows how to live and operate in the 21ˢᵗ century.

We must fight digital illiteracy, which risks 'blocking' Europe – and Italy, which is lagging behind in this area – thus making it irrelevant on the global scene. In Europe in 2016, a generation incapable of using technology is a lost generation. To avoid this, we need an intense digital educational programme. I do not use the term 'education' casually. If we consider contemporary history around the world, the greatest vehicle for removing inequality was the spread of compulsory, free, state-run schools. While schools were the prerogative only of a lucky few, society was immobilised, with gaping inequalities and few opportunities to change the status quo. With the development of the web, we risk repeating that inequality. It will only be through a widespread programme of digital education that citizens, starting with the poorest, may gain access to the full range of opportunities offered by new technologies.

This is why we must invest in the development of digital skills. Let us take a moment here examine some data: 315 million Europeans use the internet on a daily basis. But are we sure that they all use it to its full potential? According to a study by the European commission, a single digital market could guarantee €415bn of additional growth plus hundreds of thousands of new jobs. However, we still need to overcome a number of obstacles. For instance, in 2014 almost half of European citizens (44 per cent) made an online purchase from their country of residence, but only one in six (15 per cent) bought products or services online from another member state. Not to mention the fact that only seven per cent of Europe's small businesses sell to overseas markets.

Our duty is therefore to invest directly in tomorrow's European society: a society that we are determined must be more inclusive, and that can be so through digitisation. We know that digitisation can generate jobs, but we also know that 90 per cent of workers in the future will require a good level of digital skills.

We must not fool ourselves into thinking that all of this can be solved by giving a computer to everyone. That is not the point. Investment in cultural innovation is just as important as investment in infrastructure. In the Quadraro suburb of Rome, Google Italia has set up a digital gym, with laboratories and equipment, to allow local people – students, workers, those looking for employment – to learn how to use innovative technology. Such an initiative, set up by private industry but with input and support from government, represents the quintessential example of what we should do in the field of digital innovation. Thanks to this initiative, a number of unemployed young people were able to gain the digital skills they needed to apply for jobs in a variety of fields.

When I think about these issues, I cannot help thinking of that famous scene from The Matrix when Morpheus offers Neo the chance to stay in the known world or of experiencing the thrill of facing the future. A red pill or a blue pill? This may just be an image from a 1999 film, but it accurately presents the choice that lies before us today.

On the one hand, there is yesterday's world; a world that cannot change or exploit the potential that new technology and the digital world offer. On the other hand, there is a world that is just waiting to provide new opportunities and prospects for development. Are these two opposing worlds? Probably not – even if many cannot resist the temptation to pit one against the other. It is not true that the digital economy will result in many job losses. On the contrary, many blue-collar workers will have the opportunity for an improved working life, as businesses become better known and more commercialised thanks to the digital economy. Would it have been wise, 100 years ago, to stop the development of the combustion engine because it put horse-drawn carriages out of business? I do not think so. In other words, even if digital innovation leads to job losses for some – if any direct link actually does exist – stifling innovation is still wrong. The solution is to help those who do lose their jobs due to automation with the tools at our disposal now, and to equip their children with digital skills so that they may eventually form their own startup.

The reality is, and this is especially so for Italy, every day the state is moving forward and investing in innovation even when this seems impossible. Unfortunately, this is not a country where such matters make the news, because it is always easy for some to declare that the digital agenda is 'fluff' or simply 'virtual'. However, it is not virtual – it is very real, as real as anything produced by a 3D printer or an online business. The problem is that while we are preoccupied with discussing a zero-sum game of winners and losers from the digital economy, we risk not realising that, beyond the pages of our newspapers or the television talk shows, a generation that has not asked for permission has decided to go out and play. 'Startuppers of the world unite!' This should be the slogan for those who wants to invest in the future of our society.

OPENING PANDORA'S BOX

There is a provincial software company, called FacilityLive, which was established in Pavia, 40 km from Milan. Until a few years ago it was a small startup of seven people in an apartment, unknown to many, but it had great ambitions. It has now become the largest non-British company quoted on the elite programme of the London Stock Exchange (so out of the ordinary is the business, that the stock exchange did not where to put it on a map of quoted businesses, so they placed it floating somewhere in the English Channel). It is such a strong company that it has been able to turn down numerous buyout offers from Silicon Valley giants. Described as the 'anti-Google', this competitor is continuously growing, and has already received more than €32m in investment and has patents in 44 countries worldwide. In 2017, FacilityLive developed the G7 app for the G7 Italian presidency, a knowledge tool that was introduced during the leaders' summit in Taormina. Recently, FacilityLive was awarded the title of Italy's most valuable startup, with a company valuation of €225m, on the map of Europe's most valuable startups.

FacilityLive shows that one does not have to be based in California to be successful in new technology. In Pavia, the company works in close collaboration with the local university, employs 80 people (90 per cent of whom have permanent jobs) and it will employ even more now, thanks to the passage of the Jobs Act. This story illustrates that we should not fear change or the future and that, above all, we need to support our talent.

Unfortunately, when we talk about the digital single market we find ourselves faced with an obvious paradox. We know that we need to develop it; we know that it will force our economy to take a big step forward; we know that nowadays technology is the primary motor of the economy. We know that focusing on the digital market will bring many positive returns. However, despite this, we are still moving very slowly. The digital market is the challenge for tomorrow's Europeans. After so many years of slow progress, we must now pick up the pace. The Italian government is playing its part. It is not true that we are always the last to act and neither is it true that we are asleep at the wheel. On the contrary, in this field, Italy is sprinting. This does not excuse the many wasted years when we walked. But enough with the clichés. In November 2015, the Italian Digital Day was held in Turin's splendid Palace of Venaria. The record speaks for itself, looking at the series of proposals that have been implemented in recent years: the single public registry, the open data allowing increased transparency, the 'digital identity project' to simplify public services, and *OpenCantieri*, the tool through which the status of all of Italy's major projects can be monitored. It is all too easy to say that nothing ever works and that we have no prospects for the future. I am convinced that we have a future, and that it is a bright one. We just have to let it into our daily lives as soon as possible, by removing the remaining barriers that still exist.

One of the many paradoxes of the European digital market is that it is too fragmented, full of barriers that do not allow it to integrate fully and rendering it incapable of competing on the global scene. An example that illustrates this perfectly is that, like many Italians and Europeans who are passionate about soccer, I have a subscription with my cable provider to watch Champions League matches. If by chance I am away on business, I can follow a match, for example, Juventus playing Real Madrid, on my tablet. This is the case whether I am in Bolzano or 1,500km further south in Palermo. If, however, I drive an hour away from Bolzano to Innsbruck, I am not able to watch the match. Does this seem logical?

This problem is known as 'portability of content' and it clearly demonstrates the issues within the digital single market. The answer to this is to bring down this virtual barrier, one that feels very concrete in terms of my freedom. Consumers need 'portable rights' throughout the entire EU. Europe is one continent, with common institutions, functioning exchanges, physical barriers that have crumbled over time – but not when it comes to subscriptions to digital content. Partly thanks to the insistence of the Italian government, the European commission is finally looking to solve this and in February 2017 an agreement was reached. From early 2018, this absurd barrier won't exist anymore, and we will be able to listen to music, watch movies and football games in any corner of Europe, as if we were at home.

The European Union feels closer to citizens when it frees data portability and abolishes roaming fees. After years of many battles, supported by the Italian government from the very beginning, on 5 June 2017, roaming was abolished on calls and internet data. Using WhatsApp in Lisbon or Milan will cost the users the same; using Twitter, whether in Stockholm or Ljubljana, will not result in greater costs. This is another little step forward that has great impact on the everyday lives of the people. This is Europe at its best. It is the Europe we are fighting for.

It is no coincidence that one of the first international events held during the Italian presidency of the European council in 2014 was Digital Venice and the adoption of the Venice declaration. This programme was launched in Venice but has certainly not ended there. Subsequent EU presidencies have also made the development of a digital agenda one of their priorities, as other governments have followed our example.

It is a subject about which we should harbour no uncertainties. In front of us, we can see a market that is only able to exploit a very small part of its real potential. It has been calculated that a truly integrated digital market would result in a three per cent increase in GDP across Europe and the creation of hundreds of thousands of new jobs.

Currently the situation is very complex. A number of obstacles make it virtually impossible for European citizens to take advantage of existing opportunities, in terms of the goods and services that are potentially available to them.

Europe is not yet open to the rest of the world. This is why I greatly appreciated the European commission's launch of the digital single market strategy in 2015. In conjunction with the Swedish government in particular, we are working on finalising European legislation on this as soon as possible, and before 2019. I am convinced that we can succeed because, although the strategy proposes ambitious objectives, it does so within a realistic timeframe. It is not a long-term plan but a strategy based on three very clear pillars: better access for consumers and businesses to online goods and services across Europe; creating the right environment for digital networks and services to flourish; and maximising the growth potential of the European digital economy and its society, so every European can enjoy its full benefit. If we are to increase the openness of the EU, the issue of the free flow of data becomes crucial. This goes hand in hand with security, because the more secure data is, the more users will be willing to share information. I agree with the Estonian prime minister, Jüri Ratas, who, while presenting the plans for his presidency, has declared that the EU should not be based solely on the four fundamental freedoms – the free movement of labour, goods, services and capital – but also a fifth: the free circulation of data.

This is, of course, no simple task. Digital innovation requires us to make certain choices that will have a series of future consequences. We therefore need to know exactly where we want to go, because opening up Pandora's box may be risky. However, my view is that, if we wish to make a difference in today's society and, above all, in tomorrow's society, we must not hesitate any longer. When we deal with issues like intellectual property, copyright, roaming and net neutrality, the approach we must follow is to aim for maximum openness (while recognising that these are very diverse issues involving different actors and, as such, should not all be lumped together). Openness is unavoidable. We are progressively liberalising content, services and opportunity. Clearly, this means confronting some well-entrenched interests, especially those of the giants already operating in the sector, but we cannot hide and pretend that this is not the case.

The direction we are heading in will lead to better access to goods and services online. Naturally, we must find the right balance – for example, copyright must be safeguarded. But if we impose too many caveats and infinite exceptions, we will end up swimming in a sea of constraints and restrictions that will not be to the advantage of our citizens. I do not think that this should be the future that our Europe aspires to.

When we talk about digital goods and services, we should be clear that we are talking about a revolution that could disrupt to our present way of life. For the sake of clarity, I will repeat this yet again: investing in digital innovation does not mean that all our children need to become Apple or Microsoft engineers. Perhaps, we need to spread more information regarding the digital agenda, which still seems to be considered by many as an opportunity only for nerds. The reality is very different, as we can see from the experience of the Americans who, on this subject, are light years ahead. According to the latest studies, in 2013, the sharing – or gig – economy in the US was valued at \$15bn; almost half Italy's national budget. In 2025, the sharing economy is predicted to have a value of \$335bn, suggesting a growth rate of 25 per cent per annum.

In the last months of 2015, a study published by the Harvard Business Review suggested that the real crisis facing the EU was not to do with sovereign debt, immigration or the functioning of European institutions (however important these are), but a digital recession. We risk creating a multi-speed Europe and an unbridgeable gap between our citizens. On the one hand, we have those with the skills needed to benefit from the digital economy who will reap success from it. On the other, there will be those without, who are left behind. This is not the path we wish to take. Progressives must fight until the digital market is available equally to all. Through greater digital literacy we can reintegrate marginalised sections of society, by allowing everyone equal access to the opportunities derived from new technologies. Each individual will then be free to take advantage of digitisation as they wish.

Unfortunately, not all European countries are equipped to act in this way. There are certain success stories, like Britain and Estonia, but there are many who are not so successful. While Londoners are able to surf the net at breakneck speed, so much so the city has been dubbed 'digital by default', other member states are lagging behind. It has been calculated that if France were able to attain the same level of digitisation as Britain, it would derive an economic benefit totalling €100bn.

The not so remote risk is of quickly losing one's relative advantage in comparison to those countries that continue to invest substantial resources in the digital economy. Yet again, the key word here is investment. Both the EU and individual member states spend too little of their GDP on research and technology. Because of this, we must retain the European commission's objective (to spend three per cent of Europe's GDP on research and development) as a priority, even if many states are dragging their feet. Moreover, we should hear alarm bells for all those, including in the private sector, who do not invest significant resources in research and technology. A study by McKinsey has shown that the European private sector invests only 1.3 per cent of GDP on research and development. This is much less than in the US (1.8 per cent), Japan (2.6 per cent) and South Korea (2.7 per cent).

Finally, I wish to make a connection with the issues discussed in chapter four on demography. Demographic trends and digital development are related. Immigration promotes entrepreneurship, as we Italians ought to know well. A continent that is ageing as rapidly as ours should do more to encourage legal migration. We will not only derive obvious advantages concerning the sustainability of our welfare system, as we have already discussed, but also in the field of technological development. Why don't we copy the United States? A study published in 2013 by the Economist showed that 40 per cent of Fortune 500 companies were set up by immigrants and that 25 per cent of the most innovative digital startups in America had at least one founding partner that had immigrated to the US.

Making technological development a priority not only brings great benefits to that sector, but also provides a number of valid answers to other complex phenomenon, like the demographic challenge and immigration in particular. Europe's challenges require innovative solutions that are able to keep up with the pace of change in today's society – one that knows how to be more inclusive and is ready to grab the opportunities that the digital economy can offer. Am I dreaming? I don't think so. In the words of the great David Ben-Gurion: 'Anyone who doesn't believe in miracles is not a realist'.

TOWARDS TOMORROW'S EUROPE

The EU is a magnificent story of peace, liberty and progress. It was able to create unity where there was discord; it acted as a magnet for all those who were seeking a better future; and I am still convinced that it has all it needs to be the most advanced region in the world in the coming years.

However, looking at today's reality, we see Europe affected by a number of crises that intersect with, and exacerbate, each other: the economic crises and unemployment, social malaise, political weakness, growing insecurity. In short, the Nobel peace prize won by the EU in 2012 risks being a lifetime achievement award.

The EU has gone through difficult periods in its history before, but the challenges we are facing are becoming increasingly insidious. Brexit is a wound that still hurts and, even when things get better, there will not be much to celebrate. We must also consider the fact that, in a founding member state like France, the National Front polled 34 per cent of the vote in the second round of the presidential elections. In recent years, while French and Dutch voters rejected the proposed European constitution, counties like Romania, Bulgaria and Croatia chose to join. However, at the same time, many existing members have been increasingly tempted by nationalism, closed-mindedness and populism.

THINKING EUROPEAN

In this book, I have addressed some of the more important questions facing Europe today and in the future. All of these are important, but not all are central to the ongoing public debate. There is much talk about migration and Greece. Many have looked at how to address the problem of growth or security, but nobody can say that there has been a mature discussion on the management of our borders, the study of demographic fluctuations or new ways to safeguard our rights in a digital era. Politics cannot be limited to only reacting to crises and the problems we face today. Politics must be able to build a future and, to do this, we must be aware of the factors that will determine it. The ability to react swiftly to problems is not sufficient and, to make things worse, in the last decade there have been times when Europe was unable to react in a timely and effective manner to the problems of today.

Returning to acting as Europe requires us first to believe we are European. After the last few arduous years full of rescue packages, cuts in social programmes, ineffective ideas and a lack of courage, we need a new angle in our European policies. I feel that we have suffered from a lack of real political leadership. Weakened European institutions were led by a generation that did not feel that Europe was something they themselves had achieved – unlike Kohl, Mitterrand, Delors, Prodi and Napolitano – but which, at the same time, was not raised taking advantage of the great opportunities that Europe could offer, Erasmus being at the top of that list. If you don't believe me, listen to the words of the European commission president, Jean-Claude Juncker, who at the beginning of 2016 declared: "My generation is not a generation of giants but of weak successors … who forget quickly and who no longer have a direct knowledge of their own family".

A Europe of austerity, of hesitation on the big issues, of tactics and deferments, is the Europe we have seen over the last few years. A Europe that is complex and technocratic. It reacted to the financial crises with regulations so complicated that even I – someone who has studied and worked in European policy since graduating high school – had to read and re-read those 'two-packs' and 'six-packs' (the excessively complex regulations adopted during the euro crisis) of which the Ecofin technocrats in Brussels and our national capitals are so proud. But when I think that those 'packs' were drawn up, and further complicated, with the active participation of members of the European parliament, I realise how much work we have ahead of us to revitalise the EU. The reality of the Europe that we are experiencing today is quite different from the one that we wanted to create through our treaties.

When we have weak institutions and a poverty of ideas, when everything is reduced to a power play, inevitably the 'strongest' will impose its choices and its will on the others. This was often the case with Germany, which sometimes thought it could face the world alone, if it was able to create an economic space around it, modelled on its image and within which it could safeguard and promote its own interests and national strategies. The reality is quite different. Even Germany is too small to confront these global challenges alone. We can change our policies in Europe if some countries – starting with France and Italy – return to playing the role that is expected of them on the European scene. And we Italians are determined to do just this.

So the time has now arrived to ask hard and clear questions: do we still have time to save the EU? My answer is yes. We will be successful only if we manage to escape this spiral of technocracy and populism that we have been caught in during the long years of austerity. We must have the courage to stand together to confront the transnational political challenges – from growth to security – that we face. Only by proposing a completely different model to that which the nationalists promote can we win this battle, a battle that is critical to our future. We have lived with ambiguity in Europe for many years. Faced with problems spreading like wild-fire, the answer was always either nationalist or centred on singular measures that individual countries were forced to implement. Very often, politicians explained these as having been 'forced on us by Brussels' in order to hide their own national responsibility or weakness. In some cases, this was to hide the wishes of the 'creditor states' or the strong ones among them. In short, we did not want to face reality. We never really accepted the fact that the problems we were (and still are) facing are transnational in nature. When problems cross borders, they cannot be considered as national issues, or as belonging only to southern or northern Europe. When vessels arrived (or tragically sunk) overflowing with migrants, many northern and eastern European capitals considered the problem as one that belonged to Italy, Greece and Malta. Only when migrants began arriving in those countries on trains, on foot and in containers (in which some suffocated to death), did they suddenly realise that we needed to tackle this issue together. This is a short-sighted, cynical and sterile way to confront common problems. It is no surprise that it has been difficult to implement the commitments made in Brussels on border policy, the redistribution of asylum seekers or the repatriation of those who do not have a right to remain in Europe. If one sows the seeds of indifference and self-ishness, if one bases everything on idea that creditors are the ones paying the bills and therefore have the right to dictate the rules, you cannot expect the reaction to invoking the solidarity clause will be one worthy of European values or our common interests. Perhaps some of our economic and finance ministers should reflect more on what took place in 2015 and, even if they won't, we need to build a Europe that responds to our humanity, not just to our national budgets.

Thus from whichever angle one looks at this, the crisis in Europe is really the sum of a number of crises that were never tackled properly and that all lead to the same conclusion. In order to save Europe, we must radically change it. As things seem a little better right now, this is the right moment to do it. Europe needs more consensus on policies. That is the only way to change the current way of doing things.

THE CARD TO PLAY

Who can succeed in this ambitious goal of changing the way Europe works? Certainly not those who continue to preach a policy of balanced budgets! Certainly not those who take advantage of every possible opportunity to further weaken European institutions in order to derive some national advantage. It is impossible to change policies without changing those who make them. This is true even at the European level. This is why I believe that the card to play is called 'Erasmus': the European generation that feels naturally both their European and national identity. This is the only generation that really has the chance to change Europe. Their work can be continued by tomorrow's young Europeans, who are starting to take the reins of their own communities. Of course, even among our generation we find different ideas, positions and politics. I have often found myself in disagreement with Alexander Stubb, former prime minister and former economy minister of Finland. Nonetheless, we 'speak the same language'. We both know – as do many others like us – that our political actions cannot completely ignore the European dimension. To my generation, European policy is no longer foreign policy; it takes on an almost domestic quality. Only some nostalgic diplomats in our foreign ministries pretend that is not the case.

In this light, what role does Italy have to play? After too many years when we left the European pitch, our country has rediscovered an important role. Thanks to the government's reforms, Italy has recovered its credibility. From day one of taking office, Matteo Renzi refused to mince his words: "We are not introducing reforms because they are being imposed on us by Europe. We are doing so because we believe in our children." This attitude has paid off. It represents the fundamental difference between the Renzi government and its predecessors, who were immobile and inert and so ended up giving in to demands made by Brussels (and, I should add, some European capitals) as though we suffered from some kind of inferiority complex. We removed this 'external obstacle'. Italy's European decisions are now based on a mature and equal relationship, one in which each partner has its own responsibilities to carry out and that recognises all of us need to commit to reforming Europe. Here lies, perhaps, the real break with past European policy. No one is questioning Italy's European decisions, in terms of our underlying strategy, identity, values, and approach to global challenges. But Italians should no longer see Europe as an external obstacle, or use it as such. We should make decisions in view of our national interest and our vision of, and for, Europe. We should negotiate European policy with determination, in full and clear knowledge of the advantages and disadvantages that our countries will derive from them.

We must be more challenging negotiators, even difficult when needed, in order to obtain the best results possible for the Italy we love and the Europe we want. Our attitude should not be that of 'Europe is asking us to do this'. This is the wrong approach, both for Italians, as it denotes a lack of confidence in our country, and for European institutions, as we are well aware that without the votes of our government and members of the European parliament, there is very little these institutions can impose upon us. Shedding this view is a vote of confidence in Italy's abilities and is the right choice for Europe's institutions, starting with the commission.

For this reason, as well as becoming more determined negotiators, we also need to be more effective in the implementation of the policies we have decided upon and the commitments we have made in Brussels.

I want to focus a little on this, as it is what I have been working on over the past three years. Thanks to both Renzi and Gentiloni, Italy has more credit with the EU. This is due to action taken by our governments in three fields: infringement procedures, state aid, and European budget fraud. In addition, we have also saved taxpayers around two billion euros, which will be used for our citizens, businesses and the state itself. Thus, we have gained political power while also having a positive impact on our budget. I want to give you some figures: when Renzi took office in February 2014, Italy was subject to 120 infringement procedures. By October 2017, this had fallen to 64. We are no longer the black sheep, and our credibility has steadily increased. Thanks to a new approach that allows a faster dialogue with the commission, the number of procedures opened by the commission for the recovery of unlawful state aid decreased from 22 in 2014 to eight in 2017. Lastly, while there were 280 fraud and malpractice cases in 2014, there were only 158 in 2017: a better record than either France or Germany.

Things are much simpler than some media stories would suggest. Italy now has a new generation in government, one that, after many wasted years, has implemented, or is implementing, the reforms required to make the country competitive again. It is natural that some mistakes will be made along the way. As I have already suggested, politics is similar to a penalty kick. If you don't shoot, you can't score. And we need to add one more important element. These reforms are not only required to make Italy competitive again, they are also the way we present ourselves in Europe. It is now clear to everyone that, without Italy, there can be no Europe, and that Italy wants to change Europe.

Without Italy and France, the Greek negotiations would have turned out very differently, and, I fear, that the outcome would not have pleased Alexis Tsipras. A 'Grexit' in July 2015 would have been the beginning of the end of Europe. Without Italy and our presidency of the EU, nobody today would be talking about investment, and I am willing to bet that the Juncker plan would not exist. Without pressure from Italy, the European commission would never have made the issue of migration a priority and produced a co-ordinated approach.

In conclusion, the generation that began changing Italy is fighting to change Europe. It is based on a very specific idea. If I may use a musical metaphor, the Berlin Philharmonic is no longer enough to govern the EU. Not only is it not enough, but it is not right that it only plays from one score. What we need now is a European concert, where every part of the orchestra holds the final score dear. Ode to Joy is beautiful, but there are other composers other than Beethoven; there is Verdi, Puccini, Bizet. And, more than joy, Europe needs an ode to politics and to good sense – which seems to be lacking in some of our negotiations.

Metaphors aside, it has never been clearer that the only way to revitalise Europe is to change it. Otherwise, the risk of it ending up on a path to suicide is very real. We need to act as soon as possible. This current European legislature must be a catalyst for change, with deeds matching words.

The economic crises that we have been through has not only weakened European institutions (something that is serious in and of itself); the economic crises have, above all, distanced citizens from Europe. How to we regain this lost ground and bring re-engage citizens? I am not just thinking about those who have joined the ranks of the Eurosceptics. I am think of the ever-growing number of euro-frustrated citizens and, even worse, all those who becoming more and more euro-indifferent. We need to respond with new common economic policies that encourage growth and create new jobs. We need European policies that make a difference to the lives of our citizens – spreading mobility programmes, improving policies like the youth guarantee, launching new projects like a European volunteering service, taking full advantage of all the European funds available to us for the development of innovative urban regeneration policies – to name just a few examples. Italy is an important actor in this process. Now we have the duty to create political initiatives that include all our priorities – from a Europe of growth, jobs and young people, to a Europe of security, culture and the rule of law.

The challenge to change Europe is enormous. We feel this is the biggest opportunity we have ever had to bring about change. We should be honest, however. If we are unable to use this difficult moment to launch a new European policy, and not just a national one, we will be doomed to failure, and those that wish to destroy Europe with hatred and fear will prevail. They will win and, in doing so, they will deny a future to all of us. Other powers will reign while Europeans are reduced to spectators of the political games of the new century. This is why we need to think back to the successful schemes of the 20th century and rebuild them, but, above all, we must do our best to overcome the challenges of government. If we do not accept our responsibilities, if we are not ready to take risks, roll up our sleeves and get to work on revitalising Europe, the best case scenario is that we find ourselves back in opposition and, in the worst case, nobody will be interested in our ideas.

Out of all the political forces, the left has the most to lose. That the historical distinction between left and right has transformed does not scare me much. In some respects, I accept that it has softened or assumed a different meaning. Left and right, are both boxes that need to filling with values, choices and policies, otherwise they will be resigned to the history books.

The problem is a different one: that a new division is overlaying itself onto the historical distinction between right and left – pro-Europeans versus Eurosceptics. It is a divide that is evident in all European countries. Political forces are increasingly aggressive, starting with those at the extreme edges that portray themselves as anti-European, anti-euro, or simply anti-anything, and push for a return to nationalism, to the extreme right or the extreme left. They often mix ingredients from the two extremes and, buoyed by cases of corruption or bad politics in the mainstream, find the yeast they need to rise. Just think of the Five Star Movement in Italy.

This results in the fact that, more and more often, the political forces of a country find themselves pushed to the centre. Pro-European political forces are forced to defend themselves from attacks by Eurosceptics, with the result that they end up having to govern together in coalition. This happened in Germany and Italy, and there was a possibility of it occurring in Portugal after the last election, averted by António Costa's victory. It is the left, though, that has the most to lose from this forced cohabitation, as it is unable to offer a clear pro-European message and risks having to go along with conservatives, betraying its own fundamental principles. This is political suicide.

This is why we cannot resign ourselves to the status quo. We need to outline a new pro-Europe message, but we need to do so as the left. If we simply echo the pro-European right (even when they are arguably saying the right thing), how can we run an election campaign against it? How can we defend a European ideal different from that of austerity if we limit ourselves to being in only slight disagreement with the conservatives, with a campaign to marginally correct their fundamental errors?

I often hear phrases like 'the left no longer exists'. However, I am convinced that we need the left, and other progressive political forces, more than ever. At the same time, as long as we remain confined within our national borders, we will have no hope of winning elections or being able to offer an attractive alternative to the right. If we look at European conservatives, we see that all of them (or almost all) are totally supportive of austerity – from the Spanish People's party to the British Conservatives, from the German CDU to New Democracy in Greece, as well as the Dutch and Portuguese centre right.

The European left, however, is not nearly so united around any principle. Manuel Valls fought with all his strength to reorient the French Socialist party around reformist positions. But in the presidential primaries he was defeated by Benoît Hamon, who stood far from our politics, as well as from those of the majority of French voters: in the election he won only six per cent of the vote. The SPD ran a strong campaign under its leader, Martin Schulz, but it was still defeated in the German general election. The PSOE in Spain has put its faith in Pedro Sánchez, although it remains under pressure from the People's party to its right and Podemos to its left. I feel very distant from the politics of Jeremy Corbyn, who has done little as leader of the UK Labour party to avert Brexit and whose leftism seems very nationalistic. I must admit, however, that he has managed to outline a different agenda, win support from young people and, thus, obtain good results in the June 2016 snap general election, denying the Conservatives an overall majority.

In short, it will be difficult to appear credible to the electorate when we speak with many voices. Frankly, the European left is currently achieving very little. It is satisfied with its 'progressive platforms', but sadly its political agenda is without ambition or out of touch with reality. This was evident to me when I was in Budapest in June 2015 for the congress of the Party of European Socialists (PES). This is usually a very good opportunity to renew ties with friends from all over Europe. However, my overall impression was of a noticeable disengagement with the political dynamics seen in European society. Immigration, for instance, was barely discussed, mostly because of the internal divisions that exist on this subject within the PES. But this topic should unite the entire European left. Often, indeed, the international dynamics of these big European parties look more like confederations than national parties, comprised of the structures, bureaucracy and intergovernmental agreements seen in European chanceries. I believe that the time has come for the movement to break down these national barriers.

My vision for Europe would see the establishment of transnational political forces in the shortest possible timeframe. However, I am also a realist and so I recognise that we obviously need time to build these. In the meantime, we need to intensify the contact between our political leaders. Three years ago in Bologna, the then Italian and French prime ministers, Matteo Renzi and Manuel Valls, met with the leader of the PSOE, Pedro Sánchez, and the then leader of the Dutch Labour party, Diederik Samsom. Their matching white shirts were met with some mockery, but it was a very significant moment for the European left. We must reinforce and intensify the contacts between us. If required, we can recognise that we have diverging views. But, in the face of the challenges that Europe faces, we cannot limit ourselves to a pre-summit meeting prior to the European council.

In the long run, contrary to what John Maynard Keynes said, we will not only all be alive but also even more in need of a transnational European politics. If we were able to link the European elections to the choice of the president of the European commission, why can't we have real European elections with transnational lists and parties? What we need is not just a reform of government in Europe, but also a real redefinition of the European political space, with strong and effective parties to replace the weak confederation of national parties we have in Europe today.

I have always thought of Brexit not as an opportunity, but instead as an occasion to take important decisions. Britain's choice to leave the EU has put many problems on the table. What should we do with the 73 seats in the European parliament assigned to the UK? We could eliminate them all or we could share them among the 27 remaining members, thus creating disputes on how to allocate the seats. Or, we could adopt a more courageous position. In the aftermath of Brexit, I suggested allocating seats according to trans-national lists. This proposal was soon adopted by the Italian govern-ment and then by many other institutional and political actors. The French president, Emmanuel Macron, supported the proposal, and so did the French and Spanish governments. The European Liberal Democrats, led by Guy Verhofstadt, have supported it, together with the Greens and their co-chairs Monica Frassoni and Reinhard Bütikofer. The thinking behind this proposal is very simple: at present, European citizens vote in European elections on a national basis. Only a few decide to cast their votes based on their European political position. I want to stress the word European, because many voters see the elections as a way to send a message to their national politicians, instead of looking at the wider picture of the EU.

We need to reverse this trend. We must make sure that the votes are 'European votes', instead of national votes that produce effects in Brussels and Strasbourg. With transnational political lists, we could create a true European constituency. This would also be in line with the Lisbon treaty, according to which the European parliament represents the peoples and not national citizens. The constituents would then vote according to the political agenda of the party, instead of their nationality. Voters would pick the social democratic, liberal or centre-right party without looking at the passport of their candidates, and look instead at their views on Europe. The creation of transnational political lists would become the embryo of true European political parties, more efficient than the current ones.

In 2014, the candidates to lead the European commission were selected without having to go through this sort of political process.

This was a step forward from the time before the introduction of the system of *Spitzenkandidaten*,[1] when we needed an agreement between governments to select the leader of the commission. But an alternative could be to have Europe-wide primaries preceding the nomination of the candidate. In France, Italy, Germany and throughout Europe, supporters of the social democrats, liberals, centre right and so on would vote for their leader at the next European elections. It could be similar to what happens in America, with primaries that take place in the various states prior to choosing the national candidate.

The path to the establishment of transnational political forces is a long one. However, it is one we should embark upon. How can we build a common feeling between us if an Italian social democrat always feels that a German social democrat is a 'foreigner'? We must not give up in the face of this challenge. We have an obligation to think up new and innovative ideas that could revitalise Europe. And, if we cannot do this, we who were raised in Europe and who have travelled all over it, then who can?

A (DIFFERENT?) GOVERNANCE FOR EUROPE

Europe as we currently know it cannot continue to function for much longer. Europe needs a new governance. We have been arguing this, and working on it, for some time now. But, up until now, we have not won our battle over those who wish to postpone this discussion in order to maintain the status quo, or perhaps to make it worse. I am thinking of politicians like Wolfgang Schäuble, who represent the antithesis of everything we think Europe should be and of how we believe we should do European politics. From Charlie Hebdo to the Bataclan, from the Brussels airport attack to Nice and the Christmas market in Berlin, 2015 and 2016 saw direct attacks on all us Europeans. And, in the face of these tragic attacks, we must not forget the other spiralling crises – Greece, immigration, the nationalistic surges in Hungary and Poland, and Brexit.

Europeans need a more effective and efficient Europe and we need to work on this speedily. From Rome to Brussels, we have said this on a number of occasions. However, we are tired of being privately told by many political leaders how 'urgent' reform of European governance is, only to see these same people attempt to postpone to tomorrow what needs to be done today. There always seems to be an apparently good reason to postpone the debate or to limit ourselves to small-scale solutions. And so, the months and years pass and, once again, we arrive at decisions that have already been overtaken by events. For example, the decisions taken on immigration and asylum and the criticism of the Dublin treaty: it took far too much time for Europe to change its approach towards the migration issue, which was flagged as a priority by the Italian government when first in office in 2014. There was also a need to pursue reforms of the eurozone that went well beyond the proposals made in the so-called Five Presidents' Report on how to complete economic and monetary union. These were useful suggestions but were soon out of date after the final round of Grexit negotiations in July 2015. To those who say they need time to respond appropriately, our reply is that, had they started taking action at the point we originally proposed it, we would today already be much further towards a solution. This is all the more reason to stop wasting time.

The Greek crisis may seem behind us now, but I don't think we have ever come so close to Europe crumbling before us as we did during that long, all-night meeting in Brussels on 12-13 July 2015. It was a dramatic night for Greece and for all of us present. I had never before been more aware of the absurdities of the system through which the various technocrats and eco-financiers in Brussels and various other capitals exercised so much power, and in such an opaque manner. Although, in reality, no institutional or legal framework underpinned the Eurogroup. They set out 'solutions' that did not really take into consideration social and political factors, entering into tactical alliances between themselves and creating inertia and resistance in order to ensure that no outsider could 'interfere' with their very exclusive club. It was on that night that Europe's leaders came to understand this fully. The Greek crisis was about a lot more that simply the financial situation of a single country. It also made us all face the shortcomings and weaknesses of the eurozone: too little political governance, too few democratic controls, and too great a degree of economic divergence between its members.

From the very beginning of the economic crisis, the gap in levels of income, competitiveness and employment between the member states grew, along with mistrust between governments, divided between those who wanted to apply austerity measures rigidly and those who felt that supporting growth was the only way out. Distrust among our citizens was also rising. It is true that action was taken. Progress has been made to ensure more stability in the eurozone when it faces a crisis. The banking union (albeit incomplete), the European stability mechanism and the monetary policy of the European Central Bank are all tools available to us to help avoid a banking or financial crisis in one country spreading to the others.

But we cannot be satisfied, because this is still not enough. The eurozone not only requires shock absorbers, it also needs an engine. The euro is much more than just a single currency. It is also a political project, one of sharing sovereignty in order to strengthen our economies and societies and boost growth and employment in an era of globalisation. We have a duty to develop new economic and social policies in Europe. Europe has changed and the world has changed. For instance, when we built the EU, we had to ensure that a real single market allowed free competition. This was obvious but, at the time, the world was still divided into two, competition was, above all, a European and American construct. In order to create a single market we had to bring down the barriers and regulations that were used to provide state aid. Today, the world is incredibly mature and competition is no longer a European or transatlantic concept, but is global. This is why we need to rethink these policies and reinterpret European regulation. State aid – which for years was regarded with horror in Brussels – is no longer a distortion of the market, but may serve to safeguard European industry in the face of Asian or American competition. Thus, the way we apply our regulations must be revised and made less rigid. It should be more concerned with substance, and adapted to current political realities and the global economy.

In the Five Presidents' Report, the word 'convergence' appears 28 times, perhaps because the methods used in bringing about the convergence of the eurozone economies have failed. However, they failed because they were applied in a one-size-fits-all manner, requiring all the states to do the same thing at the same time. Thus, they all reduced their debt and their deficits and, to achieve this, they all first reduced investment before cutting public spending and waste. The weaker ones conducted internal devaluations, starting with cutting public-sector wages. None of them adequately invested or took all the necessary measures to stimulate demand. We should therefore not be surprised that, since 2008, Europe has taken a long slow journey out of the crisis. By contrast, the United States under Obama did exactly the opposite, meaning it was able to get out of the crisis – a crisis it was mainly responsible for – both faster and in a better condition than Europe.

It was wrong to ask the Greeks and the Finns to carry out the same measures in an effort to recover – and the paradox is that these measures were not successful in Greece or Finland. In Italy, we did not have the troika, but the harshness of the measures taken were the same, with the only difference being that Italy helped other countries to emerge from their crises while never asking for one euro in assistance from Brussels or other European capitals. Berlin seems to have forgotten this and never once explained it to the German public, just as it never set out the great advantages that Germany obtained thanks to the introduction of the euro. Some German politicians displayed more pride in their resistance to the introduction of a real stimulus and investment policy and their desire to balance our books than they did in Germany winning the World Cup. These are not complaints of a southern European. Indeed, in July 2016, the Economist dedicated its famous cover to Germany under the title, 'The German problem'. The amount of misinformation given to the German public is a political mistake for which we have all paid dearly, and which we no longer wish to pay.

One of the fundamental problems in Europe over the last few years is that it imprudently asked its member states to all do the same thing without regard to their individual situations. Until now, Europe has been overly focused on financial stability. The technocratic direction that it embarked upon led us to the worst crisis we have ever known and led us down a highway on which anti-European populist sentiment is powering ahead, seemingly without a speed limit.

To achieve a real convergence of our economies we all have to do the right thing at the same time, not the same thing at the same time. Countries like Italy and France, which have wasted too much time already, need to accelerate their reforms. Germany needs to focus on investment in its infrastructure. More widely, we must encourage growth throughout the entire eurozone, because the slowing down of large economies outside Europe will have a great impact on European exports over the next few years. Our convergence must be simultaneously economic, financial, fiscal and social. At the same time, we must govern the euro with a view to pursuing policies of growth and employment. To achieve this we have to introduce new tools and policies to encourage investment.

The journey towards European integration has taken this path many times in the past. By doubling the credits allocated to structural funds, Delors was able to convince all the member states to create the single market. It was recognised that the opening up of our markets could not be completed without cohesion and solidarity because the major advantages that the more advanced economies derived from the opening up of national markets had to be compensated with specific policies aimed at developing under-developed regions. Competition and solidarity are the twin pillars underpinning the success of Europe's markets and currency. The creation of the cohesion fund established a sustainable path towards a single currency for member states that were lagging behind. The creation of a single budget for the eurozone to provide a unified policy for growth and investment, complementing the Juncker plan and including countercyclical buffers, must now constitute a new milestone in our path to integration. We must stick to the same principles: competition, which provides more opportunity, and solidarity, which ensures equal opportunity. If we abandon either one of these, we will not get very far. And this, in fact, is why Europe is stalled today.

In order to oversee this project, we must make our common institutions more legitimate and more efficient. We can no longer call summits of the eurozone heads of state and government at the 11th hour in times of crisis. If we wish to build upon, and not just repair, the eurozone, they must be regularly scheduled meetings. And the Eurogroup must be led by a permanent president, with the power to decide on its mission statement and ensure the coherence and co-ordination of our policies. This person must not be co-opted by their colleagues, as is currently the case. They must be nominated by the heads of state and government and elected by the European parliament. In addition, in order to reduce the persistent weakness and splintering of executive power in Europe, the European commission should also have a vice-president for economic affairs.

We cannot, however, have a eurozone government without parliamentary control of the eurozone because we cannot have efficiency without legitimacy. For decisions affecting the eurozone to be more legitimate, the people of Europe need to see themselves better reflected in this new Europe. On this point, we must be very clear: either the puritans in the European parliament take a bath in the pool of reality and accept the need for the body to adapt its function, or accept the need for another parliament for the eurozone, made up of national and European politicians. I would prefer to see the former happen, but I am nonetheless convinced that some form of direct parliamentary control is necessary. Our common currency is our common asset. It is not just an instrument for exchange, nor is it an end in itself. It is one of the tools we need to fulfil our ambitions: the consolidation of a common sentiment, a shared identity, and constant solidarity in good times and bad.

Changing European institutions is not as arduous a task as it may seem. In order to begin improving the governance of Europe, we simply need to activate the clause in the Lisbon treaty dealing with reinforced co-operation. We could thus agree a protocol in which the states that form part of the eurozone undertake the task of increasing its integration. We must allow some states the opportunity to enhance their European integration without other member states imposing their veto. Enhanced co-operation must, however, be accompanied by a big increase in the level of democratic legitimacy and parliamentary oversight within the European institutions, all of which could also form part of this ad hoc protocol.

Why do we need to resort to a protocol in order to change the governance of Europe to allow some states to move forward with their integration without dismantling the current architecture? For one very simple reason. When these subjects are brought up, someone always panics and suggests that we wish to effect a treaty change. Discussion then screeches to a halt there, as though taking a walk in the park and climbing Mount Everest were one and the same.

We should be realistic. Treaty change is a huge enterprise. Personally, I am convinced that it needs to be done, but I am just as aware that there is currently no appetite for this within the EU. Even with the German elections over, there will be elections in Italy in 2018 and the ongoing Brexit negotiations. At the moment, therefore, I do not see the political conditions necessary to start working on modifying the treaties.

At the same time, however, we cannot simply put on the back burner every effort to change the status quo. The policy of taking one step forward and two steps back will not bring any benefits to the EU. The challenge, in which Italy is ready to invest political capital, relates therefore to the possibility of introducing real change in institutional attitudes in Europe without embarking on a long process of revising our treaties.

Over the course of this book, I have repeated on several occasions that we cannot remain on our current course. The eurozone is at risk of collapse and we cannot be satisfied with the supplementary, albeit fundamental, function of the European Central Bank. Do we want radical treaty changes? No. This could open up a process the outcome of which is unknown. But do we, therefore, wish to leave things the way they are? No, absolutely not. Somewhere in between the walk in the park and climbing Mount Everest lies the path we must take. I propose introducing decisive changes to improve the functioning of the eurozone in the fastest and most effective way possible. Introducing a well-defined protocol as an annex to the Maastricht treaty and the treaty of Rome, which includes predetermined, specific and necessary changes, is, in my opinion, the most practical solution. This is an idea that was also suggested by my friend Andrew Duff, with whom I have shared so many federalist battles. Such a protocol would have to contain, first of all, a clear indication of the need for the eurozone to adopt its own fiscal budget. It is not up to me, nor is it the aim of this book, to suggest figures, but it is obvious that a budget for the eurozone would have to be comparable to that of the EU (one per cent of GDP). I believe that only by the creation of a budget for the eurozone will we be able to have an EU capable of intervening in decisions regarding economic policy. It is worth remembering that, to date, the only effective solution to the economic crises was European Central Bank president Mario Draghi's quantitative easing. Juncker's commission proposed some flexibility and an investment plan to which a few billion euros were committed. These are all necessary steps but, let's be honest, a drop in the ocean. With an adequate budget, however, the European commission could implement economic policies that fight unemployment and initiate its own investment programmes. Just as Obama did in the United States, nothing more, nothing less.

It is also obvious that the creation of such a budget would also mean imposing common fiscal controls, and therefore the possibility of initiating common fiscal policies. Harmonising taxes would allow us to confront, finally, the issue of fiscal competition. Obviously, this would apply only to the eurozone. To such an economic and financial structure, we would then need to add the banking union, including real measures to ensure a European scheme to guarantee bank deposits. Without these, what kind of banking union would this be?

It is clear that this increased executive power must be balanced with appropriate counter measures. A protocol that brings about real changes must, therefore, also provide for strengthening the oversight powers of the European parliament. It has often been suggested that the problem in Europe is that of democratic control. Thus, an increase in the powers of the European executive must be balanced by a corresponding increase in the powers of the European parliament. This would mean both increased control of the commission as well as increased co-ordination with national parliaments. It is safe to say that, on issues pertaining to the eurozone, only the parliaments of countries that are members of the eurozone would be involved.

Confronting Europe's democratic question is necessary. Over the last few years, we have seen the paradox of presidents of the European council who, rather than using the existing European institutions, have undertaken their work behind the scenes with diplomatic methods inherited from meetings of the G20. The worst legacy of Herman Van Rompuy, resumed by Donald Tusk, was that instead of using existing or parallel institutions he began developing the sherpa method – where leaders' advisors meet informally, with no real controls over them, and often end up advancing proposals on crucial issues for the future of the EU. This always happens when one moves out of a transparent process and distorts the equilibrium of our common institutions. In short, we have 'sherpacracy versus democracy'. This may appear a secondary consideration, but we must work to stop us heading down a path that risks the entire system. In practice, it was the presidents of the European council – a new position introduced by the Lisbon treaty – that were the first to show a lack of confidence in European institutions. Decisions that are highly relevant to all member states and their citizens cannot be taken in secret. Both the discussions, as well as the solutions adopted, must be taken back to Europe's institutions and its traditional way of doing business, which has, in the past, achieved many important things. In more general terms, Europe must stop creating new posts which, in order to justify their existence, delegitimise the system. The experience of the first presidents of the European council confirm this. In 2019, we should entrust this role instead to the president of the commission. In this case, one is much better than two. This will avoid the proliferation of informal meetings, put a stop to pointless competition between the two presidents, end negotiating methods and decision-making processes that are opaque and parallel to institutional ones, and give the EU a recognisable face. I believe that our ultimate goal should be the establishment of a post of European president, one directly elected by its citizens. But this requires treaty change: the sooner, the better. In the meantime, we could embark on an easier road and combine the positions of president of the council and of the commission into a single post. It is time to move on.

This is why we need to reform the governance of the EU. What we have simply does not work. We face an extremely complex situation, in which the EU consists of member states with different types of membership. There are those who are members of Schengen, but not of the euro, those who are members of both, and those who are members of the EU but not Schengen, and vice versa. A new form of governance must consider this diversity, building a strong nucleus around the euro, with those who wish to increase their level of political, economic and social integration. Around this, we can form a less rigid relationship with those who wish to complete the single market, energy market and digital market, but do not wish to advance towards an 'ever closer union'. Reformed governance must be respectful towards the will of the people, as well as conscious of the EU's diversity and its opportunities. It is clear that, in order to have a functioning common market and to leave open the possibility of its expansion, it is critical that there are a good set of rules to govern it. But to have a union that is political as well as economic, rules (whether good or bad) will not suffice. We also need real transnational policies that deal with fundamental issues, and over which we cannot have the power of veto. This will create a more cohesive EU, with a solid democratic base that can legitimise its functions, and supranational decisions in areas where European action is clearly more effective than action at the national level.

We should debate this with care, ensuring that we manage our diversity without creating barriers or divisions. The EU was created to abolish barriers, not to create new ones. It has the ability to prosper, more than it already has, if it is able to construct this complex democratic system of governance.

A EUROPE BETWEEN FEAR AND HOPE

We cannot escape the fact that all Europeans are directly threatened by terrorism today. Just think of all the attacks on European soil: from Paris to Brussels, from Manchester to Berlin. However, we have rarely responded as a union, in a united way. Neither have we faced these threats as one block made up of over half a billion people.

The paradox is that those who hate us see us as more alike, and united by the same values, than we see ourselves. The problem is that those who want to destroy Europe are aiming precisely at the areas where we are divided. They are aiming at the core of our society to pit us against one another in order to weaken us and make us an easier target. This is not a time for weakness; it is a time when we need to show resolve and courage.

We need resolve and courage in the face of the terrible external threats before us, but we must also show resolve internally. If our reaction to this violence leads our societies to become less open, to an increase in racism, discrimination and other divisions, we will end up in exactly the position the terrorists want us. There is no greater challenge today than to retain our society's right to security and the security of the rights within our society, including for newcomers to Europe. We must develop a new European policy, including over defence and security, which will defend us in Europe and the world and which, at the same time, does not force us to compromiser our own values and the rule of law within Europe.

So what needs to be done? If a government is not able to guarantee the security of its citizens, starting with the right to life, then it has no purpose. But this requires us to take a big step. We will resolve little or nothing if we leave ourselves in the hands of decisions taken by individual governments, because the threat is transnational in nature. The divide between internal and external security is now outdated. Many have not yet come to understand this and prefer to adopt do-it-yourself solutions. This is not the right to confront this problem. Recent attacks may have been carried out in the French capital, but we must remember that they were organised in Belgium and planned in Syria. The killers were French and Belgian, probably trained somewhere along the Iraqi and Syrian border, as many other Europeans have been. This means that these terrorists carried out frequent trips. With each of these trips, information was constantly transiting to and from and within Europe.

How do we react to a threat of this kind? By recognising that no one country can react to this alone, while the union as a whole can. Does this mean that we should establish a European version of the CIA? This is the best solution and one that we should aim for. Unfortunately, this will be difficult to achieve right away. It is certainly necessary to move beyond simple co-operation, and we need to commit ourselves to the integration of our security and intelligence forces. Co-operation is, of course, useful. According to various observers, if the French and Belgian services had co-operated a little bit more, we would probably have discovered a lot more information about the Bataclan attack. But this requires a nucleus, for example an operations centre in Brussels, where we can work together to identify threats, prevent attacks, and come up with common security measures. If we cannot copy the CIA, let us at least try to study its best practices. For years, the United States has used the idea of 'fusion centres'. These are not actual agencies but specialised structures. Data collection is simply not enough; we also need to know how to interpret and use the data that is collected. The creation of various European fusion centres, which would have the role of working alongside national sovereign structures, thus creating synergies without abolishing existing agencies, could serve to fill an important European gap that is no longer acceptable.

Increasing controls should not automatically mean reducing civil liberties. I do not think being asked to show our identity cards or to open up our backpacks more often when we go to a stadium should pose too big a problem, if this helps safeguard our security. This is not a loss of liberty.

This is also true of the new digital age, which has brought about numerous benefits. Unfortunately, it also presents many greater dangers. Our commitment regarding this threat is very clear. We must invest in cyber security, enabling a system of web and social media intelligence. This will allow targeted investigation of the information networks used by terrorists and targeted investigations of subjects or groups who use social networks to communicate. Preventing and fighting terrorism in cyberspace must increasingly become a European responsibility. The agreement reached in Brussels on the sharing of flight passenger data is a very important example of what we can and must do. We should recognise that, every day, we voluntarily share enormous amounts of personal data, for instance, when we use our cards to shop or when we tag ourselves on Facebook. So why can't our police forces use that same information on the planes and trains we use, in order to prevent terrorism.

One area of co-operation that we need to start working on immediately is European defence and security. We have already laid the groundwork but, thus far, political will has been lacking. I am convinced we could create a European military corps, drawn from the various member states. Its members would train, work and operate together overseas. We can start working on this as groups of countries, joining our forces and equipment and developing more initiatives to integrate our militaries, increasing our effectiveness through economies of scale and showing our citizens we really can make a difference to their right to life, security and peace.

Having said this, our fight against these barbarians cannot confine itself simply to security because terrorists are not just attacking the places we live and work. They are attacking who we are and what we represent – our freedoms, rights, secularism and culture. Therefore, our opposition must also seek to revitalise the rule of law, our rights and our culture. It is not just about dropping bombs or implementing effective controls. Instead, we must respond to those who wish to stop us from publishing satirical cartoons by publishing even more of them. Whether we like them or not (personally, I am not always amused by those published by Charlie Hebdo), what is at stake here is the right to satire and the separation of state and religion. Let us therefore invest in our culture. Renzi launched a simple initiative: for every euro spent on security, we would spend another on culture. In Italy, many narrow-minded observers raised their eyebrows. But in France, someone studied the proposal thoroughly from this point of view: Italy has a huge advantage as a country of extraordinary artistic culture. These are not just empty words; our country can really play a leading role here.

Even our civil strength must form part of our response. Our leadership is derived directly from our great humanistic tradition and Europe is, above all, humanist. In response to all that is going on, I would really like to see us take one simple decision: increase the funding for the Erasmus programme by tenfold and make a period of study overseas obligatory for all European high school and university students. We should also empower the European civil service. Together with my French friend and former colleague, Harlem Désir, I launched a bilateral pilot project to develop exchanges of civil servants between Italy and France. Just think what an important project this could be if it were included all, or almost all, EU member states. Those who are convinced that they have terrorised us will find themselves faced with a generation who is even less fearful and even more tolerant. Those who want to destroy our humanity will find themselves facing the unbeatable force of our humanism.

THE EUROPE OF TOMORROW

We must also ask how we best defend ourselves from those who trade in hatred, and who appear ever more frequently on the airwaves instilling violence in the core of our society. They are political preachers, spreading the poison of violence and mistrust, exploiting our collective fears. For these fear-mongers, the solution to our various problems is very simple – build a wall. If we listened to them, we would end up with walls erected in all four corners of our continent. If we followed their advice, we would imprison ourselves within their walls and their hatred.

No, I'm sorry. Europe was not created to lock itself up. Europe was created to build bridges between people, to open those borders that were once closed, to facilitate what was previously complicated – like movement. The principles of European humanism were violated at Srebrenica and Mostar, when barbarians massacred thousands of people and wanted to blow up the Stari Most bridge, which symbolised coexistence and a meeting point between peoples and religions. Those principles were reborn through the convictions for war crimes attained at the international criminal tribunal in The Hague, and when we rebuilt that bridge in Mostar.

This same humanism must guide us today.

The immigration crisis is the third major problem to hit the EU in recent years, following the euro crises and the threat of terrorism. I remember very well all that took place following the tragedy in Lampedusa on 3 October 2013 – nothing. Hundreds of further deaths were required before alarm bells finally began to ring in Brussels. I am ready to bet that if the migration phenomenon had not reached dry ground (for how can one forget the images of Syrian refugees arriving on foot at European borders), and remained simply a maritime problem, we would have continued to hear the same response: it is southern Europe's problem. They can deal with it themselves.

This is an immense case of political short-sightedness, self-interest and indifference. It always boils down to the same fact: important transnational problems require extraordinary transnational solutions. However, for many months Europe felt that it only had to do the bare minimum and could leave the responsibility of dealing with the issue to a few member states.

For a long time, Italy bore Europe's responsibility alone. It was an enormous effort, in which we were the first to propose solutions on how to govern – instead of endure – the migratory crises and the phenomenon of immigration. This is not about vindicating our stance, but discussing an approach that is gaining traction in Europe. It is not exceptional, the premise that as the EU we should act in a united manner and share the responsibilities of a phenomenon that has swept all of Europe, rather than pass it off to a few member states. The Italian proposal, which we pushed from the start of our government, included managing the migration phenomenon, establishing a shared reallocation system for asylum seekers, increasing the funds available for maritime operations, and revising the principles of the Dublin treaty. Although largely forgotten, Italy was alone for two years before we requested the implementation of these principles. Today a number of states share our view, including Germany and Sweden. Without our work, the commission would never have arrived at its agenda for migration which, unfortunately, is progressing too slowly and which we hope to accelerate.

The Frontex agency is useful but limited, because it supports member states without any real say on how to control our external borders. The commission has taken up our proposal for the creation of a European coastguard. This agency must be assigned important tasks and become a key element in the real Europeanisation of our external borders.

We need to manage migratory flows. We cannot accept all those who arrive but neither can we turn them all away. To take one practical example from personal experience. Hosting refugees in apartments spread around cities, rather than in suburban ghettos, and involving refugees in volunteering activities is an intelligent solution that has been adopted by some more enlightened Italian local administrations, such as Catania. By contrast, becoming consumed by the urgency of the matter and concentrating hundreds of migrants in small villages or suburbs is pure folly, because it threatens those communities. We must make sure we do not repeat these mistakes, as we reap the consequences for many years. In France for example, misguided urban policies were adopted over many years in the *banlieues*, and we continue to see the repercussions of these decisions today, two or three generations later.

We have a duty to take in all those who are escaping wars. But we also have the responsibility to ask them to respect our values, which are not 'just' Italian, French or Spanish values. They are European values, the fruit of our common constitutional heritage, solemnly proclaimed by all member states: respect for our freedoms and democracy, equality among all citizens and secularism. In the past, we have been too weak in affirming the importance of our values. Sometimes we were even ashamed of being 'the west'. We should not forget the disgusting 'explanations' for terrorism that invoke colonialism only served to encourage Islamist violence against us.

We should stop this self-flagellation. Let us open our eyes and face the new challenges to our principles and values. If we do not, we will have lost before we have even started.

This is exactly where our starting point should be. Let us use our schools to teach all our children what it means to be European and what it means to be westerners. Let us teach tomorrow's Europeans that Europe is a land of opportunity, but on the condition that its fundamental principles are respected. On this, we are not willing to retreat – not as Italians and, above all, not as Europeans.

THE DEVELOPMENT OF EUROPE

Fighting both the external threat, terrorism, and the internal one, populist nationalism, is essential – but we must not forget that the current climate of insecurity and instability is the result of Europe failing to work as we would want it to. Insecurity and distrust derive, first and foremost, from the incapacity of European governments to find effective solutions to the crises that have assailed our continent.

Many European leaders agree, at least in principle, on the need to counter a resurgence of neo-nationalism by making the EU more competitive. However, disagreements arise over how to regain our competitiveness.

Betting on traditional industries, even if they are successful, is not enough. Every European economy has its strengths, and the Juncker plan is certainly a first step towards increasing investment. But this is not enough. It is not sufficient on a point of principle because it does not recognise that transformational impulse that has always animated European progress at key moments: the capacity to identify the pillars on which to build a more solid future. The left must therefore rediscover its sense of what it is capable of. It must find a challenge to which it can rise, identify its own limits, and then overcome them, just as it has done many times in the past. Take the battle for the welfare state. This was not simply one about wishing to establish better services. It was about reducing inequality and underpinning the economy during the industrial boom.

Today we are facing an analogous revolution, but this is a technological rather than an industrial one. It is obvious that technology is changing our way of life, not just our way of producing things. It is accelerating the world with the increased speed of communication making the world smaller. Its impact can be felt everywhere, from politics to society, culture to industry. Progressives must utilise this big lever if we want to remain faithful to our ideals – that is, to transform society by making it fairer.

There is no area that cannot be improved and simplified through technological advances. It can tackle many small and large problems. For instance, social services. We do not want to cut them but make them more efficient. A one-size-fits-all welfare system no longer works when we are faced with workers who move country frequently and have to deal with different work contracts and social security systems. How could we expect to adopt the same approach for everybody? Let us take the example of a young woman who started working in Italy, moved to Belgium and then went on to have a family in Britain. This, whether we like it or not, is the norm in Europe. If we want our young people to have the same social services enjoyed by their grandparents, we have to think about a different welfare system. Why has digital technology improved services in many parts of the economy, but not the public sector? This should be our point of departure: health, social security, education, energy and environmental services.

Let us take advantage of every single byte available to us in order to improve our society. Technology allows us to not only accelerate and facilitate the improvement of all services, public or private, but also to personalise them and bring them closer to the needs of the people. Here are some examples. If we provide schools with broadband, it is easier to offer and implement diverse teaching methods that fit the needs of students. If hospitals are equipped with adequate digital equipment, we can develop telemedicine, better manage the flow of patients and more. If we use technology to manage sources of energy, it is easier to understand the energy needs of families, study them and ensure those needs are met.

Energy is another important issue that a united Europe needs to confront. It may seem we should leave this subject to the experts, as is the case to some degree with digital innovation. But the reality is that, if the EU wants to play a frontline role in the global stage, it must develop a common energy policy. This should not be limited to defining where our supply of gas will come from, which is a problem facing all national governments, not just the EU. Today, even more than ever before, the issue of energy is intertwined with geopolitics, security and, above all, with the need for sustainable development and responsibility towards future generations.

Europe must not be satisfied with the status quo and must achieve an integrated energy market as soon as possible. This would allow consumers to choose freely between suppliers, while investment and research soar, thus opening up the possibility to imagine a different future for our society.

Europe has agreed to develop an energy union. This is an essential objective, as there is no other subject on which we face so many choices. Some cling to the idea of a fragmented market and polices that are not harmonised. This offers an unknown future. The transition to an economy based on reduced CO_2 emissions is unavoidable and we need to prepare for it. This could be a driver for European unity or for fragmentation, with the inevitable well-known environmental, economic and social costs.

On the subject of the environment, the European left needs to speak with a more determined voice. It needs to do so in Italy, where the green movement is too weak, in Germany, where the Greens and the CDU dominate on the issue, and in many other countries. But, above all, it must do so in Europe, where progressives must fight to ensure sustainable development. During the Italian presidency, the EU reached its first real common environmental position – a fundamental step that then allowed us to participate as a united and influential actor in the COP 21 climate change negotiations in Paris.

This should be Europe's ambition – to point the way. The Paris conference was a great success. The state of our planet was at stake. Diplomacy was conducted for months before the draft agreement was finally approved. We could discuss the thresholds, the norms, the scope of the agreement. Moreover, the EU finally played a leading role on the global stage. A failure in Paris would have been a dangerous echo of what occurred in Copenhagen in 2009, and we could not allow this to take place.

The conference also succeeded because, under Barack Obama, the US played an important role in pushing for such agreement. Donald Trump's abandonment of the agreement a few days after the G7 summit in Taormina was a sad decision with ideological roots, reflecting an isolationist vision of international politics, which will do much damage.

Now that the US want to retreat from the world stage, the EU needs to take the lead on the environment. This subject is crucial, not only because it deals with emissions quotas, but because what was at stake in Paris was how we want our societies to develop, and how we confront transnational challenges such as energy, the explosion of the global demographic timebomb, and the need to guarantee access to food and water. None of us wants to see a recession with all its negative consequences. But we also need safeguards against out of control growth in one region of the world to the detriment of others. Paris sought to achieve an equilibrium – one not just on paper – to improve the future for billions of human beings who live in unequal conditions.

In Paris, the EU proved itself a leader. COP 21 was the occasion to revitalise our work. We should now keep seeking a path to an energy union and sustainable development. This is not just about safeguarding the environment; it is also about a new attitude to guarantee jobs and economic growth.

THE NECESSARY PATH TO TAKE

Often in European history, decisions have been taken quickly. Ambitious goals are set in the belief that, during their implementation, errors, misunderstandings, and disputes could be ironed out. This was the case for the introduction of the single market, the euro and enlargement in 2004. Sometimes this approach has been necessary but, on other occasions, more time may have been required.

We must now decide what kind of EU we want and with whom we wish to build it. I have absolutely no nostalgia for the good old days, when Europe had six or nine members. And I do not share the views of those who think we should restart from that point. At the same time, however, we cannot fool ourselves into thinking that we can achieve all we want to achieve with all the member states.

Some may ask, if not the austerity approach, what exactly do we want? The answer is easy. We need to have a common European strategy for investment that helps growth, rather than depresses it. We want go back to Maastricht, when our commitment was to keep the deficit below three per cent, and to Lisbon, which includes economic and social progress as a central common objective, as well as the fight against inequality.

It is clear Italy has to face up to the issue of its public debt, not because Europe is asking us to, but because it is right to do so, and because our children demand it of us. For this reason, we have come up with tough measures to reduce debt, which will last throughout the next parliament. Our proposal keeps the deficit at 2.9 per cent, as long as we can use the additional margin to push economic growth. In this light, we would co-operate with the European commission within the framework of a 'partnership agreement': we ask for a greater margin to strengthen growth, while we commit to enact reforms, carry out investment and reduce debt.

This is our idea of Europe. Wolfgang Schäuble often talks of a tightknit group of member states that have adopted the euro. He spoke of this in 1994. I did not agree with him 20 years ago and I do not now. Many states are held hostage by divided public opinion and therefore avoid taking a clear position. But an *à la carte* EU cannot work, one in which states welcome cohesion funds but then refuse humanitarian assistance to refugees.

Europe is primarily a community of values, before it is an economic and political project. The time has come to ask whether those values are, as we thought, shared by all. On issues ranging from Greece to migration, we have seen a Europe of ultimatums and diktats all too often. From this point of view, 2015 was a year of no return. The truth is that the only thing that will save the EU is if it rediscovers its sense of community and manages to give its citizens a reason every day to put their trust and hope in it. We cannot move forward while being divided on everything and creating conflict everywhere: between north and south, between creditors and debtors. All of this is destructive for Europe.

We can regain the trust that has been lost over the last few years by making it clear Europe cannot be imposed upon us from above. The future of millions of people cannot be decided in the European chanceries – to avoid misunderstanding, this is as true for the people of Germany as it is for those of Greece. We cannot have a document written in German that decides whether Greece remains in the euro. Equally, we cannot have referendums called from one week to the next, as the Greek government did in 2015. The single currency and the single market must be governed in a collegial manner, avoiding giving one country the right to veto or, worse, the ability to impose itself unilaterally. We will not save European unity if we maintain a system of one-size-fits-all regulations that were developed in who-knows-what plan in some Brussels building.

We are facing a problem of political will. But that is not all. From the various crises we have faced, we can see that our common institutions are no longer able to produce effective results. On the contrary, more often than not we have found that these solutions produce the exact opposite outcome of what they were supposed to achieve, dividing the people of Europe rather than uniting them.

The EU is an extremely complex institution within which diversity – of values, geography and history – is the rule rather than the exception. To govern the EU, political decisions cannot be taken at the highest level and then passed down the ranks. It is now more necessary than ever to manage a series of key policies at the European level and to leave the others, which are more national in nature, to be managed by the states. Thus, the European Central Bank's decision to launch the quantitative easing cannot be examined solely by the German constitutional court in Karlsruhe. Why is a national constitutional court more important than the European parliament? The topics we discussed in this book – the European economy, migration, security, the digital agenda, demography and investment – have no boundaries or borders and therefore need transnational treatment. This is why changing our institutions is necessary – because if we do not, there is a real risk that the entire EU will disintegrate.

We need more democracy, a lot more democracy, in Europe. This is why I believe we should explore the idea of holding a pan-European referendum to decide upon the next big constitutional choices facing Europe, asking all European citizens to vote on the same day. This is the only means through which we can revive some sense of democracy and with it some legitimacy. In the summer of 2015 there was much talk surrounding the debate held in the European parliament on the Greek question when Tsipras explained his decisions. To some extent, it seemed incredible that the European parliament was debating such an important matter. But this should make us stop and think: if we do not discuss European matters as Europeans in European locations, what did we create the EU for?

Let us, therefore, discuss these matters, but let's make it a real debate. Let us lay all our issues on the table and work to rediscover the reasons why we should remain together. Let's do it now. If we delay the political choices into the next legislature, after 2019, it will be too late. The days of tactical delays and watered-down solutions is truly over.

The kind of Europe I want to see is filled with courageous political decisions. I think of Simone Veil, a 'founding mother' of the EU. I had the honour this year of representing the Italian government at her funeral in Paris. Her life symbolised the desire for the rebirth of an entire population, the people of Europe. A survivor of the Holocaust, Simone Veil fought to defend the memory of a past that she had lived. Remembering does not erase the pain, but it surely helps prevent such events happening again. We should look up to her and move forward. To do so, I think of the Erasmus generation. We should not forget that the Erasmus generation is still a precious minority. But its pioneers are now stepping onto the stage, ready to assume the increasing responsibilities for which they were raised and trained. It is from the Erasmus generation that Europe will find the founding children, those who will play leading roles in a new integration process for Europe.

The basis of this battle is as simple as it is complex. It is about facing all the upcoming challenges – the economy, migration, development, demography and security – by working across national borders. Here lies the real political challenge: surmounting national borders. We cannot fight terrorism effectively if we are unable to unite our security forces. We will not be able to resolve the issue of migration if we do not convince ourselves that the Greek or Italian borders are European borders. We cannot have a foreign policy – particularly regarding that very unstable European region, the Mediterranean – if we do not speak with one voice when negotiating with other regional actors.

A transnational strategy for transnational issues is indispensable. Otherwise, we will never have lasting solutions, only temporary fixes. This is the principle underlying our commitment: that of developing real transnational policies, made by transnational political forces, in forums of transnational politics. Within such a Europe, the easyJet generation will finally feel at home.

NOTE

1. The *Spitzenkandidaten* method was experimented with for the first time in the 2014 European elections and saw the head of the list of the European political family that won the elections become the president of the European commission. There were five candidates – Junker for the European People's Party, Schultz for the Social Democrats, Verhofstadt for the Liberals, Tspiras for the Left and Keller for the Greens. Prior to 2014 the choice of the president of the commission was left to political negotiations between the heads of state and government.

ABOUT THE AUTHOR

A founding member of the centre-left Democratic party, Sandro Gozi is Italy's Europe minister (secretary of state for European affairs in the office of the prime minister).

As a student, he was among the first to participate in the Erasmus programme, spending time at the Sorbonne in Paris. He also holds a master's in international relations from Sciences Po, where he taught for fifteen years, and a doctorate in public law from the University of Bologna.

After time as a diplomat in the Italian ministry of foreign affairs, he served as a senior adviser to presidents of the European commission, Romano Prodi and José Manuel Barroso.

A member of the Italian parliament since 2006, he served as chair of the parliamentary committee on Schengen and immigration affairs, and was responsible for EU affairs within his party before being appointed Europe minister in 2014.

The author of numerous books and articles on the future of Europe, he is a knight of the French National Order of the Legion of Honour and of the Order of Academic Palms.